WHAT PEOPL

FRE̶̶_̶̶_̶̶_̶̶_̶̶

Freedom is something everyone needs, but few ever find it. Painful pasts, harmful addictions, damaging habits, and poor mindsets—all of them are chains that wrap around our lives and rob us of our potential. Jason Hanash delivers, once again, with his latest book that lays out practical steps to obtain the freedom we all need—and want. Read this book, do what it says, and watch the power of freedom be released in your life.

—Chris Sonksen
Pastor/Author/Coach

I couldn't think of a better book for what the body of Christ needs TODAY! Jason's writing style makes it easy to discover both freedom from sin and freedom for the things of God. He is such a brilliant storyteller and dedicated practitioner that you won't want to put this book down.

—Doug Garasic
Best-selling author and Founding Pastor of Rust City Church

In Freedom, Jason poignantly and practically presents a path to experience that which God invites us all into—freedom. His compelling stories and timely insights offer a way forward for everyone regardless of the life we've lived. It's an invitation to hope again. Get it. Share it. And walk further and further into freedom.

—Dr. Jeffery Portmann
Director of Church Multiplication Network AG USA
Author of *Delayed Destiny*

While we have been tested and tried by the circumstances that construct our lives, how we confront our day-to-day often determines how these situations shape us. In *Freedom: 8 Steps to Healing and Transformation*, readers will embark on a profound journey where they are challenged to evaluate how our past hinders us from growing and experiencing true freedom found in Christ. This transformative guide offers a roadmap to healing, guiding readers through eight essential steps that lead to genuine breakthroughs and lasting freedom. With wisdom, compassion, and practical insights, Jason provides a compelling narrative that empowers anyone seeking a path to transformation. As you navigate these pages, you'll find yourself submerged in this personal journey, beyond letters printed on a blank page. Diving into this book is like going on a quest with a trusted companion—a quest for healing and deeper revelation. Prepare to embark on a life-changing adventure—one that promises not only healing but also the liberating joy of genuine freedom.

—Rich Guerra
Superintendent, SoCal Network

In my lifetime, I have met people who did not like the name given to them by their parents, so they changed their name. Maybe it's time for all of us to trade our names from what evil tries to peddle us to what God has already said about us. Jason helps us do this. If you want to experience the God kind of freedom, I recommend *Freedom: 8 Steps to Healing and Transformation.*

Or, you can continue down the same old road and fall into a hole on the way to your destiny. If you aren't proactively removing labels from your past, you shouldn't be surprised when you not only fall into one of those holes but also set up residency in a plan for your life far from

God's intention. It's all about your choice. Thank you, Dr. Hanash, for identifying those traps and showing us the way to freedom.

–Mike D. Robertson
Legacy Pastor, Visalia First Assembly

FREEDOM

8 Steps to
Healing and Transformation

JASON HANASH

ARROWS & STONES

CONTENTS

INTRODUCTION

I know this may sound over-the-top, but as you read this book and absorb these thoughts, life as you know it will *never* be the same. Really.

This roadmap to freedom is designed to challenge you to move toward truth—truth about God, truth about faith, and truth about yourself—no matter where you are on your faith journey.

It may sound redundant, but the reason Jesus set us free is so that we can live in freedom, according to Galatians 5:1: "It is for freedom that Christ has set us free. Stand firm, then, and do not let yourselves be burdened again by a yoke of slavery."

This is what it means to live—as Jesus said—life abundant. To the full. Not just surviving but overcoming and overflowing. It means living our days filled with hope, joy, and purpose. It means living our lives the way God always intended for us.

God wants a relationship with you, and He sent His Son, Jesus, to bridge the gap between earth and heaven, so you can know Him. The journey may not be easy, but it will always be rewarding.

During this season, you will decide how far you are willing to go to find freedom. There's an ancient promise found in the writings of the prophet Jeremiah that is directly on point: "If you seek Him with your whole heart, you will find Him" (Jeremiah 29:13).

DO YOU WANT IT?

When Jesus saw an invalid lying by the pool of Bethesda—a place in ancient Israel on the temple mount where the lame, sick, and blind loitered—waiting for someone to lower them into the stirred waters so they could be healed, He knew that the man had been disabled for a long time. Therefore, He said to him:

> *"Do you want to be made well?" The sick man answered Him, "Sir, I have no man to put me into the pool when the water is stirred up; but while I am coming, another steps down before me." Jesus said to him, "Rise, take up your bed and walk." And immediately the man was made well, took up his bed, and walked. —John 5:6-9, NKJV*

How would you answer the question Jesus asked that broken man?

Do you want Me to help you?

Jesus doesn't want to make us better; He wants to make us whole.

The Greek word used in that scripture for "made well" literally means *whole* or *complete*. You see, Jesus doesn't want to make us better; He wants to make us whole. In the encounter with that sick man, Jesus wanted to get the man to look deeper into his heart. The sick man's problem was that he was looking to others for help—even blaming them for his lack of healing. We can imagine the man saying, "I have no one.... They are always.... If YOU could...."

But an encounter with Jesus is never about "them". It's about you. Do you want to be whole? Do you want to be free from the prison of your mind and the strongholds limiting your life?

He is concerned with more than our problems—our infirmities or afflictions. Truth be told, He is not really concerned with external circumstances, though we seem to obsess over them. God's concern is about what is inside us—our inner life. In order for us to get anywhere close to whole, we must find victory on the inside. Only then can we radiate it on the outside.

In the journey of healing and transformation, it is crucial for us to address the roots of the tree in order to bear the fruit of the Spirit. Just as a healthy tree depends on strong and nourished roots, our spiritual growth and the manifestation of godly behaviors and results are dependent on dealing with the deep-seated issues beneath the surface.

If we don't deal with the root, we won't get the fruit.

It is tempting to focus solely on external behaviors, trying to mold ourselves into what we think a Christian should be. However, true transformation starts from within. It starts by identifying and uprooting the underlying causes of our ungodly behaviors and replacing them with the truth of God's Word. If we don't deal with the root, we won't get the fruit.

The roots of our struggles can be found in various areas. They can lie in past hurts and wounds, unresolved conflicts, negative thought patterns, or even deeply ingrained sins. These roots have the power to choke and hinder the growth of the fruit of the Spirit in our lives.

Dealing with the roots requires courage and vulnerability. We must be willing to dig deep into our hearts and examine the areas that need healing and transformation. This involves seeking God's guidance, allowing the Holy Spirit to reveal areas of brokenness, and being open to receive His healing and restoration.

As we confront the roots and allow God to work in us, we begin to see the fruit of the Spirit flourishing and maturing. Love, joy, peace, patience, kindness, goodness, faithfulness, gentleness, and self-control become evident in our lives. These fruits are not the result of our own striving or efforts but the beautiful outcomes of a heart that has been surrendered and transformed by the grace and power of God.

When we deal with the roots, a complete transformation takes place. Our attitudes, thoughts, and behaviors align with the nature of Christ, and we become vessels through which God can work mightily. We are freed from the bondage that once entangled us, and we experience the abundant life that Jesus promises.

In the journey of healing and transformation, let us not neglect the roots of the tree. By dealing with the root, we position ourselves to bear the right fruit—fruit that brings glory to God, impacts the world around us, and fulfills our purpose as children of God.

A JOURNEY OF TRANSFORMATION AND HEALING

While we consumed by our circumstances God is more concerned with our character. Even if the circumstances don't change, and the people around you stay the same, God wants to change you. I want to invite you on a journey of transformation and healing. A journey of experiencing the freedom that is yours in Christ can be found in 8 Steps:

Step 1: The journey begins as we face the pain of our past. The baggage we are still carrying around from yesterday's wounds and experiences.

Step 2: Identifying the labels we have put on our self and allowed others to put on us and discover our true identity in Christ.

Step 3: We'll have to choose between religion and relationship and realize that they are harder to distinguish then we actually thought.

Step 4: Identifying the generational curses, mindsets, and habits that were passed on to us and breaking them in the name of Jesus.

Step 5: Learning to discern and respond to God's voice leading us in our own life. True freedom is found in the presence of God, "and where the Spirit of the Lord is, there is freedom" (2 Corinthians 3:17 NIV).

Step 6: Mastering our minds and our thought life. No longer allowing the enemy to rule our inner life through deception—but taking captive every thought and bringing it into the obedience of Christ.

Step 7: We will learn how to live separate in a culture full of idolatry that seeks to rob us of our freedom and inheritance in Christ. The world has a brand of freedom, but Jesus says, "So if the Son sets you free, you will be free indeed" (John 8:36 NIV).

Step 8: We'll learn to use spiritual weapons to fight a spiritual warfare.

If you are ready to be made whole, your life may indeed never be the same. Your pursuit of freedom and all it means and brings begins today!

DEALING WITH THE PRISON OF OUR PAST

Our human capacity to remember can be like a two-edged sword. Some memories can bless us, but others seem to haunt us.

Nearly 180 years ago, a man walked the nighttime streets of London, England, and dreamt up a story. When he was ready to put pen to paper, he wrote six words that would change the literary world: *"Marley was dead, to begin with."* Of course, the writer was Charles Dickens, and the story was *A Christmas Carol.*[1] It was published on December 19, 1843, but sold out by Christmas Eve. Within a year, Dickens' little story had gone through thirteen printings.

Too many people relive their own version of the Charles Dickens classic, complete with their own haunting ghosts of Christmas Past.

Many of us live like kids hiding in our beds with the blanket pulled up over us. We lie there paralyzed by shame, regret, and fear-driven guilt. Memories become barriers to personal and spiritual growth, keeping us angry, bitter, and distrustful. We try to bury those painful

---

1 Paulette Beete, "Ten Things to Know about Charles Dickens' A Christmas Carol," *National Endowment for the Arts*, 4 Dec. 2020, www.arts.gov/stories/blog/2020/ten-things-know-about-charles-dickens-christmas-carol#:~:text=A%20Christmas%20Carol%20was%20first,editions%20of%20A%20 Christmas%20Carol.

memories, but like emotional zombies, they keep coming back to taunt and haunt us. Jeremiah knew all about the ghosts of his past. Tormented by memories, he said,

> *"I remember my affliction and my wandering. The bitterness and the gall. I well remember them, and my soul is downcast within me."* —Jeremiah 3:19-20

He remembered obsessively. He knew God was going to come to the rescue because he had been the chosen messenger to share that news with the people. He had written about how the Lord was going to prosper the nation and give them a hopeful future, despite the current era of judgment and deprivation. But the prophet was stuck in the past. All he could remember was affliction, bitterness, and gall.

He was saying, in effect, "Look, I know God is going to rescue His people, but I haven't seen it yet. If the past is prologue, the story doesn't get any better."

Like Jeremiah, many of us have a hard time believing in a hopeful future because we remember too much. We're haunted by ghosts from our past.

THE GHOST OF PERSONAL TRAGEDY

Terrible things happen every day in our world.

As morose as this is, I've heard stories of unthinkable loss (as I'm sure you have, too). I heard of a story about a guy who wanted to propose to his girlfriend in a fountain, but when they stepped in, they were electrocuted. Parents suffer the loss of children. The list goes on and on, but when these tragedies take place, it's easy to retreat into a dark place of depression and sorrow.

Personal tragedy often leads us to a place of *doubt* and *distrust* of God. We know God is all-powerful, yet tragic circumstances come around, and we find ourselves doubting Him and losing our capacity to trust Him. When this happens, our ability to trust *anyone* in our lives is short-circuited. The inability to trust others is an obvious threat to healthy relationships. The ghost of personal tragedy loses its bearing on your life when you cling to this truth: the freedom you received in Christ is not freedom *from* tragedy, but freedom from the *impact* of tragedy that keeps you sunk. While the former may *seem* more attractive, I want to challenge you to think twice. What kind of freedom would you really have if God prevented all tragedy on the earth? Think about it this way. How would a child know the depth of his parent's love for him if he is living a perfect life, never in need of support or rescue? True love is demonstrated *in* hardship, not *without* it. Without it, we are automatons—all the same, with the same perfect experiences, with the same perfect relationships, with the same perfect lives. That's not really freedom.

THE GHOST OF PERSONAL FAILURE

This is what Jeremiah meant in Lamentations by "my wanderings"—those times when he strayed from the right path. We have all known the pain that comes from bad choices—when someone fails to say "no" to drugs, drinks too much, and then maybe gets behind the wheel. Or how about losing our temper and hurting someone else with our words—or worse? A choice was made, and damage was done—maybe irreparably.

Bad choices have consequences. We reap what we sow. It's as real as the law of gravity. Relationships are lost. We become estranged from those we love the most. And it haunts us. Soon, we become consumed with our lives in an effort to dampen the pain and self-hatred. We build defense mechanisms and box people out of our lives. We punish ourselves; walking through life almost as if Jesus, the One who was punished, was only punished on behalf of everyone else except for us. You're not an exception to the rule—and if you think you are, then you are actively denying the freedom from shame and guilt that is yours for the taking. This leads us to another ghost from the past.

THE GHOST OF RELATIONAL WOUNDS

This is what Jeremiah was referencing when he remembered the bitterness and the gall. This is a big one because we live in a world populated by imperfect people. People can be hurtful, usually because someone has hurt *them*. It's a vicious cycle. Maybe someone has lied about you—or to you. Maybe you've been stabbed in the back. These things happen in all sorts of relationships, from marriages to the workplace to the closest of personal friendships.

When you hold on to your history, you do so at the expense of your destiny.

It can even happen in the church.

And when we don't deal with the wounds that come our way, we give way to bitterness and vengefulness. We want someone to suffer because we've suffered. These desires can rear their ugly heads at the most unexpected times and most unexpected ways. Here is an important thing to bear in mind: When you hold on to your history, you do so at the expense of your destiny. Rather than moving forward in the freedom

Christ has given us, we hold ourselves captive to memories of betrayal and hurt—either inflicted on us or by us.

Our ghosts are born out of three toxic roots that short-circuit our capacity to grow beyond our past and into the freedom to thrive in the midst of adversity.

Unrealistic Expectations

We want Earth to measure up to heaven, but it never will. We should never lose sight of the fact that Jesus came into the world to rescue—but not yet. The world is full of trouble. This has been the case throughout human history. One of Job's friends reminded him that "man is born to trouble as the sparks fly upward" (Job 1:7, ESV). We think there's going to be some point when God is going to love us so much better than everybody else that He will allow us to skip some of the bad stuff.

But it doesn't work that way.

And Jesus told His disciples that as they lived in the world, they would have tribulation. (See John 16:33.) It's an inescapable fact of life. One day, Jesus will save us *from* the world, but for now, we need to let Him save us *in* the world. We must focus like a laser beam on what Jesus said immediately following the part about having tribulation in the world: "But take heart; I have overcome the world" (John 16:33, ESV). Unfortunately, we often toil to accept tribulation instead. Our expectations remain unfulfilled because they are unrealistic, and so we settle into disappointment that brands our future.

Untreated Pain

We all have this dark capacity to tuck the pain of misfortune away so we won't have to deal with it. I suppose it's a function of our desire for self-preservation, but if we don't process pain in a healthy way, it has a way of acting like a time bomb that will explode. It produces unresolved yesterdays.

Sweeping things under the rug is a prescription for ruining a bright future because it delays reconciliation and repair. Things go unresolved for protracted periods of time—sometimes years.

You may have heard the saying, "Time heals all wounds," but it's not true. Only the Holy Spirit can heal you. So, when we try to put our skeletons in the closet, it's only a matter of time before they escape and come back to haunt us.

Proverbs 28:13 says, "He who conceals his sins does not prosper, but whoever confesses and renounces them finds mercy." Hiding our past doesn't heal it; it only explodes.

We tell ourselves things like, *Life's tough. Just deal with it. It's no big deal.* However, it actually is a big deal, and it requires careful attention. But we must make sure not to get pious about it. False piety can make us put on masks and act like nothing is wrong. Why is it that Christians think admitting a struggle is unspiritual? Pretense in the face of pain is like trying to stop a hemorrhage with a small Band-Aid—too little and always too late. How can we find healing if we can't even face the pain? It's denial at its most deadly.

There is a great illustration of this from the game of golf. When you hit the ball on the fairway just right, you make a divot—a little piece of turf. What you're supposed to do is fix the spot immediately. The idea is to retrieve the displaced grass and reinsert it in its original place, patting it down with your club or foot. Sometimes, a golf course will provide some seed to add. This must be done *right away.* The damage must be fixed before taking another shot.

Why?

Because the divot will regenerate in a matter of a day or two if fixed *immediately*—before it has time to dry out. If, however, you walk away and leave it untended, it will exponentially prolong the time needed for regeneration. It's the same when we get hurt. Our instinct is to wallow in self-pity—spending an inordinate amount of time obsessing about the unfairness of it all. But this is not just an exercise in futility; it also ensures a more difficult and distended recovery period.

The prophet Jeremiah knew a thing or two about this. In fact, he indicted an entire generation of pretenders. He said in Jeremiah 8:11, "They dress the wound of my people as though it were not serious. 'Peace, peace,' they say, when there is no peace." You may be trying to show others that all is "peace" with you while you are actually over-whelmed by untreated pain. The truth is, when we are hurting it's not the time to try to be super-religious.

Instead, we must resolve our yesterdays or else: "In your anger do not sin: Do not let the sun go down while you are still angry, and do not give the devil a foothold" (Ephesians 4:26-27).

Anger begins as a reflex—an almost involuntary response to irritation. Feeling anger is not sinful, but *unresolved* anger can become sinful because it makes us more likely to do something that will hurt us and others. That's sin.

It's like when one of those dashboard lights comes on in our car. Something needs to be fixed. But we tend to ignore it until it's too late. Then there's a breakdown. That's exactly what can happen when we have unresolved yesterdays. Paul also said something ominous in his letter to Ephesus. He told them that failure to resolve issues in a timely manner gives the devil a foothold. In other words, we let our guard down and become vulnerable to a devilish punch in the mouth.

Unhealthy View of Self

If you're constantly living your life with your only assessment of yourself being your assessment of yourself, you're going to walk around imprisoned by a wrong perspective. We need to learn to see ourselves as God sees us—through the prism of His love and sacrifice for us. I love how *The Message* renders Romans 12:3: "The only accurate way to understand ourselves is by what God is and by what He does for us, not by what we are and what we do for Him." The real view is God's view. That's a life-changing truth, and it can chase away all feelings of insecurity, inferiority, and feelings of inadequacy.

Unrepented Sin

Please note, I did not say *unconfessed* sin. Just because you acknowledge the sin and confess it doesn't really mean the same thing as *repenting* from it. Repentance means to change direction. It's more than just feeling sorry for something. It's turning around and moving in a new direction.

If we don't fully repent of our sin, it causes us spiritual and emotional pain. King David was a textbook example of this. He described what he felt because of his failure to repent:

> *When I kept silent, my bones wasted away through my groaning all day long. For day and night your hand was heavy upon me; my strength was sapped as in the heat of summer. —Psalm 32:3-4*

Note the descriptive language—"my bones wasted away," "groaning all day long," "your hand was heavy on me." It's the graphic picture of a man imprisoned by his past from unrepented sin.

So, how do *you* want to deal with your past? You have a few options.

YOU CAN BEAT YOURSELF UP

Too many followers of Jesus live a life consumed by guilt, but that guilt is not from God. It's a direct denial of the cross that set us free. I suppose we think that beating ourselves up is some kind of penance. We feel we need to pay for what we've done. It's a tool used by the enemy to neutralize us. He wants us to exhaust ourselves by trying to tread water in a shark-infested ocean of guilt. Guilt is his specialty. It is his most effective fiery dart. The very word "devil" means "slanderer." He loves to hurl accusations against us. It's who he is:

> *And I heard a loud voice in heaven, saying, "Now the salvation and the power and the kingdom of our God and the authority of his Christ have come, for* **the accuser** *of our brothers has been thrown down, who accuses them day and night before our God."*
> *—Revelation 12:10, ESV* (**emphasis added**)

I don't know about you, but I've never known anyone to pay penance after being absolved of a crime. What if you heard a story in the news of a man acquitted from second-degree murder who was then sentenced to twenty years? That makes no sense! You, my friend, are the acquitted criminal. If you are sitting in guilt, then you have voluntarily walked into your own prison cell, locked yourself inside, and thrown the key off the edge of a cliff. You better go find that key!

Guilt brings spiritual paralysis. It tempts us to despair of any possibility of real change and progress. We begin to think, *I'm never going to be able to conquer this problem. The stain will never go away. Why even bother to try? Why fight it?* And that kind of guilt-driven thinking strangles us and drags us down. We hate ourselves. But that kind of self-loathing is not of God.

The bottom line is this: You can't change your past, but Christ can change your future.

We need to understand the fundamental difference between guilt and the always constructive conviction of the Holy Spirit. Guilt seeks to destroy us. Conviction seeks to grow us. Big difference. Guilt beats us down. Conviction raises us up. Guilt breeds a spirit of hopelessness. Conviction leads to confession, forgiveness, cleansing, and refreshing: "If we confess our sins, He is faithful and just and will forgive our sins and purify us from all unrighteousness" (1 John 1:9).

Almighty God makes the deliberate decision to limit His memory when it comes to our sins and failures because sin is an event. It isn't a person. When we received Christ, everything changed, and because of that, we can change everything: "Anyone who belongs to Christ has become a new person. The old life is gone; a new life has begun!" (2 Corinthians 5:17, NLT)

The bottom line is this: You can't change your past, but Christ can change your future. In fact, He already has. He has given us the choice to believe Him. He has given us choice because choice is freedom.

There is a popular prayer written by a well-known Lutheran theologian in the days following World War II. The theologian's name was Reinhold Niebuhr. He wrote the prayer that is quoted and used so often and by so many people. You have likely heard it, but I'd like you to linger on it for a moment. It's called "The Serenity Prayer," and it says: "God, grant me the serenity to accept the things I cannot change, courage to change the things I can, and wisdom to know the difference."[2] Do you see the fingerprints of choice in that request? Can you accept without choosing to accept? Can you change things without choosing change?

YOU CAN BLAME OTHERS

This one can be tricky because sometimes other people contribute to the bad things we have done. People hurt us, and it becomes like a splinter in our finger. If we don't deal with it, infection can fester. It can get exponentially worse. Swollen. Red. Painful. Someone may brush against it or accidentally touch the infected area, and you immediately bark at them. "*Why did you hurt me!*" But the real problem is that we let it go unresolved for far too long.

We love to shift blame to others. It gives us temporary relief. But it doesn't take long for bitterness to set in. We lash out at others when the problem is really in the mirror.

> *See to it that no one falls short of the grace of God and that no* **bitter root** *grows up to cause trouble and defile many. See that no one is sexually immoral, or is godless like Esau, who for a single meal sold his inheritance rights as the oldest son. Afterward, as you know, when he wanted to inherit this blessing, he was rejected. Even though he sought the blessing with tears, he could not change what he had done.* —*Hebrews 12:15–17, NIV* (**author emphasis**)

This whole blame thing has been around since the beginning of the human story—the Garden of Eden. Adam and Eve ate the forbidden

---

2 Reinhold Niebuhr, "Prayer for Serenity." *Prayer for Serenity // Faith at Marquette // Marquette University*, www.marquette.edu/faith/prayer-serenity.php.

fruit. But when confronted by God, both of them placed the blame elsewhere. Eve blamed the serpent, and Adam actually blamed God for giving him the woman as a companion. I want you to hold on tightly to this: when you blame others for your own decisions, you ensnare them in a prison of guilt and shame, and when you ensnare others in that prison, you ensnare yourself. See where this is going? In one point of the finger, you have robbed two people of freedom—not just one. When you fail to recognize your God-given freedom, it spreads like an infection. When you choose to smother the smoke of your imprisonment that is choking you out, you give yourself and those you come into contact with the fresh air of freedom.

YOU CAN BELIEVE GOD

This, of course, is the correct and healthy way to deal with the failures that can haunt us. We need to believe that He sees us differently than we see ourselves, and we need to start seeing ourselves through the prism of that relationship rather than the prison of our own thinking. The enemy has sold us a bill of goods—a pack of lies about us. And we buy into what he's peddling so easily. He wants us to see ghosts everywhere.

But we need to turn on the light—God's light!

God has this profound way of turning all your negatives into glorious positives. God rewrites our past, transforming it into a completely different narrative: "You planned something bad for me, but God produced something good from it" (Genesis 50:20, author paraphrase).

Joseph was, in that short verse, telling his brothers, the very men who had sold him into slavery and caused him so much pain for such a long time that they had hurt him deeply—just as they had intended. But he also told them that he had learned something through his sufferings. He learned that God would use all sorts of life experiences, the negative and the positive, to develop our character and work out His plan for our lives. If you can remember that the next time someone hurts you or apply it to someone who has already hurt you, it will change your life.

FINALLY BREAKING FREE FROM OUR PAST

The journey to freedom begins with something Jeremiah wrote. It's a breath of fresh air from an otherwise depressing lament, a blade of green grass springing up through the ground that has been scorched by an immense fire that consumed everything in its path. I really believe what the Weeping Prophet had to say must become one of our go-to reminders:

> *Yet this I call to mind and therefore I have hope: Because of the Lord's great love we are not consumed, for His compassions never fail. They are new every morning; great is your faithfulness.*
> *—Lamentations 3:21–23*

We have to get rid of all the ghosts. We must stop letting the enemy's dossier of our flaws, faults, and failures define us now and in the future. When we fail to release the past, we empower it to control our future. When we don't forgive someone because we're convinced that by doing so, we are empowering a hurtful person, we're believing a lie.

Here's the takeaway: God enjoys letting us off the hook.

Please remember—forgiveness is actually self-empowerment. There is power in forgiveness. Liberating power. Wonder-working power. Bitterness keeps power away. Grace and forgiveness bring it back where it belongs. It's like the prophet Isaiah said in Isaiah 43:18: "Forget the former things; do not dwell on the past."

God's forgiveness of us is not the end of the story. Not at all. Jesus didn't just come to forgive us. He came to do something even greater. He came to cleanse us—to completely remove the stain. To completely remove the guilt and shame. He came to renew our lives as if those bad things never happened. He came to redeem us. He came to release us:

> *He does not treat us as our sins deserve or repay us according to our iniquities . . . as far as the east is from the west, so far has he removed our transgressions from us.* —*Psalm 103:10-12*

You may be hiding in your bed with the covers pulled up over your head, but God says, "It's not there. There's nothing haunting you. It's gone. I removed it. You need to buy into my truth and see yourself as I see you!" I love how the prophet Micah puts it: "Who is a God like you, who pardons sin and forgives the transgression of the remnant of his inheritance? You do not stay angry forever but delight to show mercy" (Micah 7:18).

Here's the takeaway: God enjoys letting us off the hook.

God wants to do something new inside us. In fact, He wants to give us a new heart. No surgery, bandages, or patchwork but a completely new muscle, as it says in Ezekiel 36:26: "I will give you a new heart and put a new spirit inside you; I will remove from you your heart of stone and give you a heart of flesh."

He is not going to let the past become scar tissue for you to build protective walls around. All you need to do is partner with Him. God says you're free. But you are only free if you think you are free.

It's like what Jeremiah told the Israelite nation when it was gripped by hopelessness. He spoke on behalf of the Lord: "For I know the plans I have for you . . . plans to prosper you and not to harm you, plans to give you hope and a future" (Jeremiah 29:11).

That's the picture He paints for you—His vision for you. It is how He sees you, no matter how you see yourself.

There's a reason fixating on our past hurts our present, and it goes beyond the experience of pain. It becomes who we are (or who we think we are). It mislabels us as misfits and victims rather than as children of God. If we don't believe we are God's children, we won't act like it.

We have to let God re-label us, because the labels of our past mark us as slaves to the world—like the orange jumpsuit of a prisoner. That's not a good look! Let's dive into step two of our freedom journey, the re-labeling process and begin to clothe ourselves with who we really are—free and victorious in Christ!

KNOWING MY TRUE IDENTITY

"The tongue has the power of life and death."

—Proverbs 18:21

Do you read labels? They help us understand the side effects of our medicines, the ingredients in our food, and how or where things—from clothing to cars—are made. But some labels—at least a particular category of them—don't help us at all. In fact, they can hurt us deeply.

I'm talking about how we label ourselves.

What do you believe about *you*? What does the conversation going on all day in your head sound like? Do you find that you are frequently upset with yourself? Do you call yourself names?

Labels can liberate or confine us. They can grow us or beat us down. When we use negative labels about ourselves, they tend to be self-fulfilling. But it can be the same with positive self-labels. There is a common idea in psychology called the Pygmalion Effect, named after a character from Greek mythology. The idea is that high expectations lead to more productive performance, while low expectations have the opposite impact.

We need to counteract and overcome labels that hinder our growth and happiness. These labels represent things we believe about ourselves that are just plain wrong, and they keep us in bondage—completely at the mercy of our old identities. When you think about it, a label is like a bad tattoo on the psyche. It is something that becomes almost engraved on our hearts. We believe the lies and act out accordingly.

Will you ask yourself a question and give yourself a moment to really think about it?

WHO AM I?

Does your mind go to your career? Or maybe you think about family history as the core of your identity? Do you think of your gender, your successes and achievements, your failures and mistakes?

Or maybe we are like the chameleon, acting one way when we're at home and another way when we're at school. Maybe we act one way when we're at church and another way when we're in the world.

A lot of us have allowed the world, our circumstances, and our influences to dictate who we are, and we walk around confused about our identity. One of the most famous examples in the Bible of a confused identity is the story of Moses. In the book of Exodus, the people of Israel were slaves in Egypt, and the Pharaoh was afraid of how numerous they were becoming. So, not only did he enslave them, but he committed infanticide by drowning every male born among the Israelites in the Nile.

By God's providence, Moses was rescued. His mother put him in a basket and sent it floating down the Nile on a prayer. That basket found Pharoah's daughter, who took the baby in and spared his life. This is a story of lost identity. Confused identity. Missing identity. It's the story of how Moses rediscovered who he really was, how it changed his life, how it changed his destiny, and how it changed history.

> *By faith Moses' parents hid him for three months after he was born, because they saw he was no ordinary child, and they were not afraid of the king's edict. By faith Moses, when he had grown up, refused to be known as the son of Pharaoh's daughter. He chose to be mistreated along with the people of God rather than to enjoy the fleeting pleasures of sin. He regarded disgrace for the sake of Christ as of greater value than the treasures of Egypt, because he was looking ahead to his reward. By faith he left Egypt, not fearing the king's anger; he persevered because he saw him who is invisible.*
> *—Hebrews 11:23-27*

Once you know who you are, you will be able to stand firmly against stress. You will be far more resistant to the pressures of this world and closer to Jesus. Your fulfillment in life increases and your fear in life decreases when you know exactly who you are.

There are four things that knowing your identity will do for you.

Knowing Your Identity Demonstrates Spiritual Maturity.

Let me say it this way: The road to spiritual maturity leads to personal identity. What does that mean? The closer you get to God the more you're going to understand who you truly are because God is your Creator. The more you understand your Creator, the more you're going to understand why He created you.

When you are spiritually mature, you stop asking that "who am I?" question and that "What am I supposed to do with my life?" question. Growing up, Moses asked all the questions that everybody will eventually ask themselves in this life. We all ask these questions growing up: Who am I? Where did I come from? Where am I going? Does my life matter? Does my life have meaning? Those are all identity questions.

Hebrews 11:24 says, "By faith Moses, when he had grown up, refused to be known as the son of Pharaoh's daughter." Here's a guy who's born a Hebrew slave—the poorest of the poor—no clout, no influence. He was raised in the palace of the most powerful man in the ancient world—Pharaoh. You couldn't get further apart in economic and social strata. Moses had to ask himself, "*What am I going to be? Royalty or a slave?*" Moses was experiencing an identity crisis.

You need to start telling yourself, "I'm a product of my past, but I'm not a prisoner of my past."

Which one would you choose? Would you fake it for the rest of your life and be somebody you weren't really meant to be? Or would you be who God made you to be? Moses was a man of integrity. He refused to live a lie. And it's living that lie that's causing so many problems and pressures in your life. Much of the stress in your life comes from not knowing who you are. When you don't know who you are, you live for the expectations of others. You live for the approval of others. You live in the fear of rejection of others. You become a people pleaser instead of a God pleaser.

This is what Jesus, who is the most spiritually mature person of all time, said in John 8:14, "I know where I came from and where I'm going." I want you to get to that point. I want to help you get to the point where you're saying, "I know who I am, and I know where I came from, and I know where I'm going." That is spiritual maturity.

You know who you are, and you know who you aren't, and you don't try to be who you're not. You know what God made you to be and you know what God didn't make you to be. You know what your past is, and you don't lie about it. You don't fake it. But you don't run away from it either.

You need to start telling yourself, "I'm a product of my past, but I'm not a prisoner of my past."

Yes, you have a past. Some of it is good, some of it is bad, and some of it may be flat out ugly. But your past is the past. It's over with. It can't control your future. It is not your destiny. Your past has passed. Your future is your destiny.

Knowing Your Identity Defines Your Responsibility.

Here's what I mean: when I know who I am, I am clear on what God expects of me and doesn't expect of me. I've learned that God doesn't expect me to do certain things. God doesn't expect me to lead worship. One day when I stand before God, He's not going to judge me for gifts He didn't give me.

So, when you know who you are, you know what your responsibility is, and you know what your responsibility isn't. That's so important because it relieves stress in your life. God custom-made and planned all of the events around Moses' life in order to prepare him for the assignment of delivering and leading his people. He wanted Moses to be the national deliverer of Israel. So, everything that happened in Moses' life was designed to set him up to do that.

God didn't design Moses to be an artist.

He didn't design him to be a rock star.

He designed Moses to be Israel's deliverer.

His plan for Moses was to first be born a Hebrew slave. He gave him the right parents because He knew the exact DNA that was needed to make Moses. He planned that his parents would not raise him. Instead, God's plan was that he would be raised in royalty. In the Egyptian palace. Both of those things were part of God's plan to prepare Moses—born a Jew but raised Egyptian. That would make the perfect combination for a national leader.

When Moses finally learns his real identity—not as Pharaoh's grandson nor even an Egyptian—but a Hebrew, a Jewish slave's son—he immediately understands his assignment, mission, and purpose. He can no longer ignore the cries of people in pain, and he accepts his mission and his responsibility. Look at Hebrews 11:25, "Moses chose to be mistreated along with the people of God rather than to enjoy the pleasures of sin." He chose it.

In your life, if you're going to be who God wants you to be, you're going to have to make some choices. There's going to be some things you have to say no to. And there's going be some things you have to say yes to. Did you notice when this happened to Moses? Verse 24 says, "when he had grown up." We have to grow up.

Knowing Your Identity Determines Your Priorities.

Knowing who I am helps me know what to focus on and what to ignore. When you know who you are and who God has made you to be, you intuitively understand what matters and what doesn't matter, what to prioritize and what not to prioritize, and how to spend your time and your money. It helps you establish your priorities.

Think about Moses. Born a Hebrew slave, raised in a life of luxury as Pharaoh's grandson. He saw all these slaves being beaten and murdered, wasting away and starving to death, as they built pyramids and the Egyptian infrastructure. He saw how hundreds of years of slave labor built the land of Egypt.

He could have said, "I've got plenty of excuses to ignore those people and their pain. Really, it's none of my business. Besides, I have palace priorities. I'm the grandson of Pharaoh. And on top of that, I'll work within the system to make change for justice and against racism . . . and stuff like that."

No. Once Moses knew his true identity, it changed his priorities. Suddenly, the stuff in the palace doesn't matter anymore. How do we know that? Look at Hebrews 11:26, "He regarded disgrace for the sake of Christ as of greater value than the treasures of Egypt, because he was looking ahead to his reward."

We want to change our circumstances. God wants to change us.

When it says, "Moses regarded", that's a judgment call. It means to evaluate, to consider, to weigh in the balance. Moses made a value judgment. Moses gave up the same temptations in Egypt that plague us today—popularity, pleasures, and possessions—because he knew his true identity.

Moses decided that fulfilling God's purpose was better than popularity.

He decided that loving God's people was better than pleasure.

He decided that having God's peace was better than possessions.

How was he able to do that?! "Because he was looking ahead to his reward."

What I look at is what I'm going to become. And what I look at most is what I'm going to love the most. My vision determines my values. And Moses was a man of vision. He looked ahead to his reward. Paul had the exact same vision. In Philippians 3:8, he says, "I consider everything a loss because of the surpassing worth of knowing Christ Jesus my Lord."

All the stuff I used to have, the life I used to live—none of that is worthwhile anymore compared to the priceless gain of knowing Jesus.

Knowing Your Identity Determines Your Destiny.

Your identity determines your destiny. Once Moses realized who he was, his life took a whole new direction. You know what the problem is? We want to change our circumstances. God wants to change us. We're so excited about changing our circumstances. We think that if we can just get away from this relationship, if we can just get away from this home, if we can just get away from this environment, then we'll be happy.

My joy is not determined by what happens to me, but what Christ is doing in me and through me.

The problem is that when you move, you take you with you. See, my joy is not determined by what happens to me, but what Christ is doing in me and through me.

Hebrews 11:27 (NLT) says, "It was by faith that Moses left the land of Egypt." Notice that learning your true identity does two things. It gives you the courage to let go of the past. It was by faith that Moses left the land of Egypt. And it gives you the courage to walk into the future. It continues: "not fearing the king's anger, He kept right on going because he kept his eyes on the one who is invisible."

When asking the question, "Who am I?", let's look to what God says for the answer. Colossians 3:1-3 says, "Since, then, you have been raised with Christ, set your hearts on things above, where Christ is, seated at the right hand of God. Set your minds on things above, not on earthly things. For you died, and your life is now hidden with Christ in God."

The Scripture declares that our identity is in Christ. You must abandon any image of yourself that is not from God. You must start believing what God says about you. Finding your identity in Christ means believing that what God says about you is truer than what anyone else says, including yourself.

There's a great story in the Book of Genesis that's about identity, involving a woman named Rachel. When Jacob saw her for the first time, it was clearly a case of love at first sight, but that's where the fairy tale ended. Their story was a long one with many twists and turns. When they were finally together as man and wife, Rachel struggled with fertility issues while desperately wanting to give Jacob children.

Eventually, she gave birth to a son. They named him Joseph. Then she became pregnant again, but when it came time to deliver, she had difficulties. In fact, her own life was in peril during labor and delivery. When the baby was born, her midwife told her not to despair because she had another son, and with her last breath, Rachel named her baby boy Ben-Oni which meant "son of my sorrow". Her husband Jacob renamed their son Benjamin which meant "son of my right hand". He relabeled his little boy to remove the stigma of sorrow and pain. Can you imagine having a name that basically meant "my momma died giving birth to me"?

Now, you really can't blame Rachel for giving her little bundle of joy such a bummer name. She was not only in pain—she was grieving. She was heartbroken. She'd never feed her tiny baby. She'd never see her son take his first step. She'd never see her boy grow up and have children of his own. She lived such a disappointing life, and then just when it was all taking a turn for the better, she had to leave it all behind.

Jacob didn't want the boy to grow up under a cloud of grief and gloom. He wanted his son to have a label that meant something positive, something that spoke about their relationship, and most importantly, a name that was prophetically symbolic of our future as children adopted into sonship through Jesus Christ—seated with Christ at the Almighty's right hand in heavenly places (Ephesians 1:19-20) as we share in the life of Christ (Romans 8:11). After all, back in those days, the very mention of a right hand was synonymous with the idea of blessing. Our identity as God's adopted sons and daughters, by definition, means that the spirit of slavery is no longer ours to carry (Romans 8:14-15). Translation: we were freed from the orphan label.

By the way, years later, Jacob would go through his very own relabeling—but from God Himself. After the patriarch wrestled with the Angel of the Lord, God gave him a new name—a much better one. You see, the name Jacob meant "supplanter or deceiver". As a young man, he seemed to wear it as a badge of honor. He was labeled as a liar and manipulator, so he acted that way. He was a con artist and fast operator. But God had a new name for him to grow into and act on—Israel, which meant "my God prevails".

You see, when God speaks into your life, it's never about your past—it's always about your *future*.

He doesn't identify you by the painful things you've experienced. He identifies you with a new purpose. If you've been carrying around a negative label—a soul tattoo that marks you as some kind of failure—you need to find a new label from Him. In other words, you need to prophesy truth over your life—speaking forever truths—not right-now realities or past circumstances. If you have been internalizing a negative label based on lies or half-truths, or if you have bought into something that's inconsistent with the reality of how God sees you, then you need a new label:

> *You are a chosen people, a royal priesthood, a holy nation, a people belonging to God, that you may declare the praises of him who called you out of darkness into his wonderful light. Once you were not a people, but now you are the people of God; once you had not received mercy, but now you have received mercy.* —1 Peter 2:9-10

The process of applying new labels to your inner dialogue begins with identifying those areas where negative labels have been engraved on your heart, and then asking the vital question: *How does God see me?*

The apostle Peter nailed it. He said we are "a chosen people", "a royal priesthood", "a holy nation", and "a people belonging to God". Those are powerful truths and glorious thoughts, and they can be the basis for transformative internal labeling. Let me share five labels we should proudly wear as a badge of honor—nametags for easy and rapid identification—as a free child of God.

I AM COMPLETELY ACCEPTED

When we don't feel accepted, we can't be released from the prison of rejection. Some of our deepest wounds come from rejection. Too many of us go through life with this label. We feel discarded and like we are damaged goods. Maybe it began with your family years ago. Maybe it has to do with your career and how your coworkers see and treat you. Maybe it began back in school. Possibly, you've been rejected by a person who was once a close friend—or even a spouse. The simple fact is that you really can't be betrayed by an enemy—only by a friend.

Whatever the origin of your rejection label, you find yourself on a persistent quest for acceptance. You want to belong. You want to feel loved. It becomes a major life pursuit, then an obsession. Soon you are chasing it. And when you are desperate for it, you can find yourself looking for acceptance in all the wrong places. What you are doing is holding *yourself* captive to the opinions and judgments of man—judgments that will always fall short of the Truth and will *always* leave you feeling inadequate. If you are drowning in the feeling of inadequacy, you can guarantee that the fear of man is behind it.

When you think about it, we can do some crazy things to earn acceptance. Have you ever looked at photos from your life decades ago? You may find yourself asking, *What was I thinking?* Of course, we were following the crowd and trying to fit in. That's the only possible explanation for things like bell-bottom pants, mullet haircuts, and long sideburns.

All because we want to be accepted. And here's the thing: while many will love you across your lifetime, many will reject you. Don't glue yourself to something that you will never escape.

When I was in the fifth grade, I had my friend ask a girl if she would hang out with me on the school playground and be my girlfriend (I was too afraid to ask myself). But when he came back from talking to her, he told me she said, "My mama said to say no to drugs." Ouch.

My schoolboy crush instantly turned into a crushed schoolboy. I vowed then and there never to ask a girl out ever again. I was devastated. The pain lasted for weeks. Then I decided to ask that girl's best friend out, thinking, *I'll show her.* My rejection led me to do something hurtful. It's true—hurting people hurt people. Remember chapter one? Your prison of rejection will be someone else's prison of punishment.

Stop chasing acceptance everywhere else. It's a gift from God. You can't earn it. You must receive it.

Remember sports in school? There is always a kid who is picked last—or not at all. Everyone wants to be wanted. Some of you can remember it like it was yesterday. Your inner voice was saying, *Don't pick me last. At least pick me second to last.* All of us have been last at something, and we've worn that rejection label. Maybe we still do. Things like that can haunt us and hurt us even years later.

Now, think about the flip side of that. Doesn't it feel wonderful to be chosen by someone you love? Doesn't it feel great to get that promotion or reward? Isn't it good to have someone affirm you? Well, I've got some cool news for you—you have been chosen by God Himself—before there was anything else! And when you get a hold of that idea, you are ready to start the process of turning into a whole new you as described in Ephesians 1:4: "He chose us in him before the creation of the world, to be holy and blameless in his sight by his love."

Paul put it this way in his letter to a pastor named Titus: "Jesus treated us much better than we deserve. He made us acceptable to God and gave us the hope of eternal life" (Titus 3:7, CEV). Ultimate acceptance comes from God through the finished work of Jesus Christ. Stop chasing acceptance everywhere else. It's a gift from God. You can't earn it. You must receive it. How do you receive it? You choose it. You say yes. Start saying yes to God more often and watch the chains of the fruitless chase of acceptance fall.

That's where your new identity starts.

I AM EXTREMELY VALUABLE

If you thought ultimate acceptance was great—wait until you grasp this next concept. God not only accepts us, but He also values us. That's what Peter meant when he wrote, "You are a holy nation, a people belonging to God." This means that we are priceless to God. To be holy means to be separated unto God. It's the idea of being "set apart".

We call some real estate in the Middle East the "Holy Land", meaning it's a special place—set apart. In the temple, there was the "holy of holies", a separate place—set apart for God. You get the idea. Contained and implied in the idea of being holy is being of value. We are valuable to God because we are "a holy people to the Lord . . . God . . . His treasured possession" (Deuteronomy 7:6).

When God looks at us, He doesn't cringe and think, *I created that?* Not at all. He sees us as His treasured possession. The prophet Isaiah wrote that God says, "You are precious to me" (Isaiah 43:4). Has anyone ever called you precious? Maybe your parents, but I doubt anyone else has called you that—at least not with a straight face.

But God sees us as precious, priceless, and extremely valuable.

I AM ETERNALLY LOVED

We know this because Peter made it clear that we belong to God: "Once you were not a people, but now are the people of God" (1 Peter 2:10).

We have this new identity, and it has profound implications. We are part of His family. Do I need to tell you how complicated family dynamics can be? The famous novelist Leo Tolstoy began his classic 1887 novel, *Anna Karenina*, with these words: "All happy families are alike; each unhappy family is unhappy in its own way."[3] Haunting, but so true.

I'm sure some of you reading these words have been hurt and disappointed by family. Or, at least, there is some aspect of your family that you are embarrassed by—maybe even ashamed of. When you are tempted to focus on that, focus instead on the fact that you are eternally loved. See, your freedom is an eternal promise. With eternal love comes eternal freedom.

The prophet Jeremiah gives us two important truths about the love of God. God says, "I have loved you, my people, with an *everlasting love*. With *unfailing love*, I have drawn myself to you" (Jeremiah 31:3, NLT, *author emphasis*). What does being eternally loved mean? It means that God's love for you is everlasting—it literally will never end, no matter what. It means that God's love is unfailing—His love will never let you down; it will never fail.

I AM TOTALLY FORGIVEN

In Romans 8:1, the Apostle Paul assures us of this transformative reality: "Therefore, there is now no condemnation for those who are in Christ Jesus." These words resound with a profound resoluteness, reminding us that through our faith in Jesus, we are liberated from the grip of guilt. Our slates are wiped clean, and we stand justified before the Creator of the universe.

Isaiah 43:25 reinforces this truth as it declares, "I, even I, am he who blots out your transgressions, for my own sake, and remembers your sins no more." The words of this ancient prophet echo through the ages, illuminating the heart of our gracious and loving God. Not only does

3   Leo Tolstoy, *Anna Karenina* (London, England: Penguin, 2001).

He forgive our sins, but He intentionally chooses not to remember them. We no longer bear the weight of our past wrongdoings because God has cast them off, freeing us from their burden.

Embracing the reality of being totally forgiven means acknowledging that our sins and mistakes do not define us. The mercy and grace of God have transformed our identities. We are no longer prisoners of condemnation and shame but rather children of the Most High, clothed in the righteousness of Christ.

Understanding this truth allows us to let go of self-condemnation, self-punishment, and the need for approval from others. Our worthiness is not determined by our past actions but by the all-encompassing forgiveness of our Heavenly Father. We must learn to see ourselves through God's lens, as vessels of redemption and vessels of love.

By grasping the concept of being totally forgiven, we can finally exhale the heavy burden of guilt and inhale the liberating breath of God's unconditional love. We can stand tall, confident in the knowledge that our sins have been cast away and replaced with God's divine grace.

Dear reader, today, I encourage you to embrace the truth of your total forgiveness. Meditate on Romans 8:1 and Isaiah 43:25. Let these verses be engraved upon your heart, reminding you that you are forgiven, loved, and embraced by the God of second chances.

As you journey forward, remember that the road may still be marked with stumbling blocks and moments of weakness. But take solace in the truth that your identity as one who is totally forgiven remains unshakable. Embrace this reality, and let it transform every aspect of your life, bringing you into a deeper relationship with the One who offers true freedom and abundant life.

Our worthiness is not determined by our past actions but by the all-encompassing forgiveness of our Heavenly Father.

I AM FULLY CAPABLE

While it is essential to embrace the truth of our total forgiveness, as Christians, we are also called to recognize the inherent capacity that God has given us. Every believer has been endowed with unique gifts, talents, and abilities, making us fully capable of carrying out God's purpose and mission on this earth.

In 1 Peter 2:9, we read: "But you are a chosen people, a royal priesthood, a holy nation, a people belonging to God, that you may declare the praises of him who called you out of darkness into his wonderful light." This verse speaks of the priesthood of every believer, affirming that each one of us has a unique role to play in advancing God's kingdom. We are not merely spectators but rather active participants in God's redemptive plan. Remember the metaphor of the prisoner? Prisoners cannot participate in the works of humanity—not necessarily because of an innate deficiency in skill or talent, but because they are not allowed to leave their prison cells. This is the same for you, but the difference is your prison door is wide open. You can walk out whenever you want. God has already made you capable; He's fully equipped you with everything you need to accomplish what He has destined for you to accomplish.

This capacity to carry out God's plan is not rooted in our own strength or abilities but rather in God's power working in and through us. Paul reminds us in 2 Corinthians 3:5-6 (GNT):

There is nothing in us that allows us to claim that we are capable of doing this work. The capacity we have comes from God; it is he who made us capable of serving the new covenant, which consists not of a written law but of the Spirit. The written law brings death, but the Spirit gives life.

These verses reassure us that our capacity is not limited by our natural talents or skills but rather by the supernatural presence of the Holy Spirit. It is through this divine empowering that we are transformed from mere mortals to bold ambassadors of Christ.

We must recognize that God has given us all the tools we need to fully carry out His mission, including spiritual gifts, wisdom, and discernment. By embracing this truth and embracing our identity as capable children of God, we can overcome any obstacle and accomplish great things for the kingdom of God.

As you go about your life, remember that you are a chosen and set apart priesthood, fully capable of fulfilling God's purpose in your life. Your capacity comes not from yourself but from the Holy Spirit, working in and through you. Embrace this truth and allow it to propel you into a life of renewed purpose, passion, and freedom.

Here is the reality of who you are in Christ, and I pray you receive it:

I AM RELABELED

What's true in the moment doesn't have to be true in the future. This profound statement holds a key to unlocking the transformative power of embracing your true identity in Christ. Too often, we allow the labels imposed upon us by society, past experiences, or even our own self-doubt to define who we are. But dear friend, I implore you to cast aside those limiting labels and open your heart to the truth of being relabeled by the One who knows you fully and loves you unconditionally.

In the eyes of our Heavenly Father, you are not defined by your failures, weaknesses, or mistakes. He sees you as a masterpiece, intricately woven together for a purpose that transcends all boundaries. God sees the potential within you, the person you have been created to become, the completed state that lies beyond your current circumstances. He is not limited by your flaws or setbacks, for He is the God of second chances and limitless transformation.

Embracing the reality of being relabeled means surrendering the false narratives that have held you captive and adopting a new perspective rooted in God's truth. It means refusing to accept the labels of "unworthy", "broken", or "defeated", and instead embracing the labels of "loved", "redeemed", and "victorious". It means standing boldly in the truth that you are a beloved child of the Most High, chosen and called for a purpose that only you can fulfill.

It's time to shed the old labels and embrace the powerful reality that God has relabeled you. Allow His truth to seep into every fiber of your being, transforming your thoughts, actions, and perspective. Remember, what's true in the moment doesn't have to be true in the future—for the Author of your story is still writing, and His plans for you are filled with goodness and hope. Embrace the truth of your relabeling and step into the fullness of who you were created to be.

Now that we are beginning to understand our identity in Christ, let's move to step three in our freedom journey, and learn how we should approach, relate to, and see our Heavenly Father, and discover why this is vital to our freedom.

CHOOSING RELATIONSHIP OVER RELIGION

There is no freedom in religion. In fact, Christianity is not a religion, and Jesus didn't come to start a new one. Freedom can only be found through a relationship with Christ. This makes Christianity a new breed; a first of its kind. And because of that, it was difficult for new Christians in the days of the early church to remain in relationship, and not drift again toward religion.

It should come as no surprise to us that the New Testament was originally written to and for *new* Christians. And a man named Paul was used by God to write much of it. He was a man of both thought and action. He was an activist and a deep thinker. Though he was a Jew, he felt called by God to take the gospel to the Gentiles, something that was quite groundbreaking at the time.

Paul traveled through the area now known as Turkey preaching, bringing people together, planting churches, and training leaders. He did this from one city to the next. But no matter where he was working at any given moment, he never forgot about those he'd already helped. The people left behind were always on his mind and ever in his heart. He wrote letters to them. We call them epistles today. They were both personal and profound. And he would keep his ears open for any news about the work of the gospel where he had been before. The news would sometimes bless him, and other times it would upset him.

Like when he heard about what had happened in Galatia. That really pushed his buttons. So, he wrote a letter to them—we know it as the book of Galatians. In the first chapter, we read,

> *I am astonished that you are so quickly deserting the one who called you to live in the grace of Christ and are turning to a different gospel—which is really no gospel at all. Evidently some people are throwing you into confusion and are trying to pervert the gospel of Christ.* —Galatians 1:6-7

In the Greek language, the idea of being "astonished" literally meant that Paul was frustrated and fed up. He had taught them all about grace and freedom. But that teaching had been undermined by others who promoted law and bondage. He had taught them that being a Christian was all about a relationship with God. It was a matter of *grace*. But others had an agenda that emphasized religion. It was a matter of *law*.

And that was a *different* gospel.

There are still two primary ways to approach God. Though the hot-button issues seem to change from era to era and generation to generation, they all boil down to two gospels. One says "God has done;" the other says, "We must do." To those who think this way, grace is never—and has never been—enough. They want to complicate things. In another letter—to Corinth—Paul addressed the new Corinthian Christians who had begun drifting from the truth of the gospel: "But I fear, lest somehow, as the serpent deceived Eve by his craftiness, so your minds may be corrupted from the simplicity that is in Christ" (2 Corinthians 11:3, NKJV).

That's what was happening in Paul's day. People came along and basically said, "You're doing it all wrong. It's important to believe in Jesus, but in order to be a real part of the Christian club, you need more of the law." And the big law of their time had to do with circumcision.

The Jewish custom was for a male child to be circumcised on the eighth day. It was something designed to mark their covenant with God dating back to days even before the law was given to Moses. All the way back to Abraham. The problem was that the region of Galatia and the majority of the places where new churches were springing up was overwhelming Gentile. So basically, what these peddlers of a different gospel were saying was "the Gentiles have to become somewhat Jewish to be saved." And the best way for a man to do that was to be circumcised as an adult. As a side note, this is also the first time human language incorporated the word, "Yikes!"

This debate about law and grace fueled the first theological problem for the church. The idea of including minor surgery (minor unless you were the patient) as part of a membership class was understandably controversial and polarizing. I'm sure those membership classes were largely made up of women. I picture the men dropping their wives off to church. "No, honey, you go ahead. I'll wait outside."

Things got so bad that they had to have a big meeting to resolve the issue as recorded in the book of Acts chapter 15. They put their minds together in Jerusalem to think through the issue of a religious gospel versus a grace-centered gospel.

It seems that there is nothing new under the theological sun. People are still struggling with this today. Many Christian denominations started because of debates over these issues. People found Jesus and freedom and forgiveness but were then encouraged to move forward on the basis of behavior. At one point in his letter to the Galatians, Paul framed the issue this way: "How foolish can you be? After starting your new lives in the Spirit, why are you now trying to become perfect by your own human effort?" (Galatians 3:3, NLT)

This is a foundational issue, not just for our personal lives, but for the entire kingdom of God. As Christians, we are to be the brand. And because of how easily Christians seem to slide back into a religious gospel, it should come as no surprise when I say that we have a major branding problem. Branding is about identity. The idea is to develop and promote a particular feature or image. For example, The Bible tells us that we should do everything for the glory of God. (See 1 Corinthians 10:31.) And I've heard what that means described this way: "To be the best possible advertisement to the world of who God is and what He does."

See the problem?

Years ago, I was grabbing a bite at an airport as I waited for a connecting flight. Not far from me sat a man who was also eating. He was drinking. Many beers. He was pounding them. We talked a bit and, sure enough, he asked that common question: "What do you do for a living?"

Now, to be brutally honest, when I get that question there is part of me that thinks of being less-than-truthful. The conversation could veer in a couple of directions. Either it will start some kind of theological debate, or I might wind up dealing with a hater—someone with a blazing dislike of religion, particularly religious leaders. But in this case, I decided to be forthright. "I'm a pastor," I said.

The guy's body language changed. He looked at me and seemed suddenly disgruntled. After a moment, he said, "Well, Pastor, I don't like Christians."

I was taken back a little, but I wanted to engage him a little, so I said, "Yeah, me too."

He smiled and said, "Wait—you're supposed to like Christians."

"No," I said, "I understand where you're coming from because I know the kind of Christians you're talking about." I was trying to get him to think about the particular "brand" of Christians he's been observing. Now he was completely confused. So, I started to talk to him about the branding problem in much of American Christianity. I said, "A lot of people have twisted it—they've perverted authentic Christianity and have turned it into what we call religion. They make it about how we can get to God instead of what the gospel is really about."

"And that is?" he asked.

"It's about having a relationship with the one God sent to us," I replied. Then I added, "So, I understand what you're saying." The look on his face told me he still didn't get it. I looked at the food he was trying to eat as we talked. "You know what," I continued, "God came to us and he paid our debt. He picked up our tab." By this time, I was on a roll and thinking I was going to pay this guy's bill and lead him to Christ, right then and there. I pointed to his food as I said this.

He looked at me and must have been thinking I saw his beer because he reached for it and raised his glass. "Well, what does your God think about this?" Then he sort of shoved the beer near my face.

I said, "I don't think God cares too much about that right now. I think He cares more about you."

"I've never heard it put like that before," he said.

I replied, "Well, it's right there in the Bible."

See, God will always choose grace over your sin.

THE TREE OF GODLINESS VS. THE TREE OF GODLESSNESS

How should I approach God and serve Him? This is a great question for us to ponder. Of course, when you think about it, similar issues apply to other religions. They all have unique pathways to God (however they define Him). They involve what people need to do to get from where they are to get to God.

But Christianity is not just another religion, though so many seem to want to treat it that way. They make it about "dos and don'ts" and rules and regs. But it never works. That's dead religion. It can be deceptively subtle. Are you pursuing goodness and godliness? Most of us want to shout the answer, "Yes!" But the better question is, are you pursuing God?

There is a difference.

In fact, this is one of the core messages of Christianity. It's foundational. So much so that it shows up in the first pages of the Bible:

> *Now the LORD God had planted a garden in the east, in Eden; and there he put the man he had formed. And the LORD God made all kinds of trees grow out of the ground—trees that were pleasing to the eye and good for food. In the middle of the garden were the tree of life and the tree of the knowledge of good and evil.*
> *—Genesis 2:8-9, NIV*

God put a choice in front of Adam—two trees. Now, many of us bring our Sunday School mindset into how we understand this ancient story. We see Eve with long hair covering her body and she's holding an apple with a bite taken out of it. But the Bible never says it was an apple. And most of us look at this as when they rebelled against God and went their own way. But there is much more to the story.

Adam and Eve had a choice, one that led them to sin, but that wasn't their intention. It wasn't what was dangled in front of them. In fact, it was a different choice in front of them—one that was much more deadly. There were two trees in the middle of that garden—the tree of life and the tree of the knowledge of good and evil.

And whenever we eat from the wrong tree and choose the wrong gospel, we experience loss and shame.

So, it was about a knowledge base—it was a worldview:

And the Lord God commanded the man, "You are free to eat from any tree in the garden; but you must not eat from the tree of the knowledge of good and evil, for when you eat from it you will certainly die." —Genesis 2:16-17

They were created for grace and designed to flow freely with God. But they were also commanded not to let the tree of the knowledge of good and evil become their worldview. That tree was not how to get to God. It was a tree that could cost them everything—even their very lives. It's a tree that can kill. It will make you reject the truth and put you into a religious tailspin. It's a tree that destroys any capacity to have a real relationship with Him. This is how legalism gets fed.

The devil didn't appeal to Eve to be rebellious. He appealed to her desire to be godly.

God wants us to have a relationship with Him, but the devil has another agenda. He wants us to miss the possibility of a real relationship with God. And he complicates things when he joins the story:

Now the serpent was more crafty than any of the wild animals the Lord God had made. He said to the woman, "Did God really say, 'You must not eat from any tree in the garden'?" The woman said to the serpent, "We may eat fruit from the trees in the garden, but God did say, 'You must not eat fruit from the tree that is in the middle of the garden, and you must not touch it, or you will die.'" "You will not certainly die," the serpent said to the woman. "For God knows that when you eat from it your eyes will be opened, and you will be like God, knowing good and evil." When the woman saw that the fruit of the tree was good for food and pleasing to the eye, and also desirable for gaining wisdom, she took some and ate it. She also gave some to her husband, who was with her, and he ate it. Then the eyes of both of them were opened, and they realized they were naked; so they sewed fig leaves together and made coverings for themselves. —Genesis 3:1-7

The devil was described as crafty. He began with a question that was designed to confuse Eve. She got defensive and then doubled down, adding her own spin about being commanded to not even touch the tree and its fruit. But the devil continued and told Eve she had heard it all wrong. She wouldn't die from eating from the tree of the knowledge of good and evil, but in fact, she'd be enlightened and become like God. The devil didn't appeal to Eve to be rebellious.

He appealed to her desire to be *godly*.

Most people think the devil is all about aggressively enticing us to sin, trying to trip us up with obvious markers of evil. But remember, the Bible describes him as crafty. His message was (and is), "This is how you get to God. This is how you become a better you. You can control your own godliness. You won't die. You are in control."

And like so many people today, Eve bought it.

She ate the fruit and gave some to her husband. Then the same thing happened to them that always happens when we choose the wrong worldview. Their eyes were opened, but they had lost something. They experienced fear and shame. Innocence was gone. That is what always happens when we eat from the wrong tree. Right after this in Genesis 3:11, God asked, "Who told you that you were naked?" They weren't supposed to know that. He created them to be free and in a relationship with Him. And whenever we eat from the wrong tree and choose the wrong gospel, we experience loss and shame. It's a foundational story, but even more, it's a foundational truth.

And we need to understand it.

Let me explain the difference between the two trees and our two choices in three ways.

1) What We *Do* Versus What Jesus Has *Done*

One way to think about this is through our Bible reading habits. How many of us read it because we want to, as opposed to because we think we're supposed to? I mean, you get your five chapters in, but then you think about a friend who is now reading eight chapters a day. You think maybe that friend has a better relationship with God than you do.

If we could just read more, pray more, witness more, take on more at church, or even give more money, we would be godlier. Now, don't miss my point—those things can indeed be the fruit of a godly life—but they are never the root.

Godliness happens when we put our focus on what Jesus has done. Period. It's not about long prayer marathons or reading through the Bible several times a year, or any other "spiritual" activity. It's how much of Jesus you can find in those activities. It's about knowing Him. Reading the Bible should be about looking for Jesus in all the right places. Pursuing Him. Hungering for Him.

It doesn't matter what mountain you're on, just as long as it's with Him.

Some put off a vibe that they have a deeper understanding of the Word than others do. They boast about great insights, but it's not really about godliness, even though they come off as if they've cornered the market on spirituality. Be careful about people like that, and definitely don't use them as models.

Jesus is our model. And he told the super-religious people of His day that being a dedicated Bible student has nothing to do with godly living:

> *You study the Scriptures diligently because you think that in them you have eternal life. These are the very Scriptures that testify about me, yet you refuse to come to me to have life.* —John 5:39-40

Don't make the mistake of confusing memorizing details about Jesus with knowing Him and walking with Him. It doesn't matter what mountain you're on, just as long as it's with Him.

Get things in the right order. God's Word is good and vital to our lives. But we need our relationship with Him to drive us into its truth. You will never find freedom from suffocating religion apart from a relationship with Him, and that requires something very simple: just letting Him love us. As He said, the scriptures are about Him.

And we should also be about Him.

2) Focusing on Getting His Approval vs. Receiving His Love

During my time in the first pastoral position I ever held, I found a whole bunch of tracks and brochures in the office I had been given. One was really old and showed God on a throne, like Abraham Lincoln at the memorial in Washington, D.C. There were humans in front of the throne who looked like little ants. It was a scene designed to evoke fear before an angry God. And I think that's how many people view God.

A national survey found that 31.4 percent of Americans believe God is authoritarian and angry at everyone's sins.[4]

---

4   Catholic News Agency, *"Majority of Americans See God as an Angry Judge, Says New Survey,"* CNA, 12 September, 2006, https://www.catholicnewsagency.com/news/7599/majority-of-americans-see-god-as-an-angry-judge-says-new-survey.

You don't need to change to get God to love you. He loves you so that you can change.

If you get the right view of God, you'll see He is not mad at you. In fact, there is one verse that describes God on His throne as laughing. (See Psalm 2:4.) You don't have to appease His anger or even win His approval. Why? Because He already loves you. That should be our focus. His love already exists, we don't have to somehow make Him love us or impress Him to look kindly on us.

God knows your sin and still loves you. He doesn't like what we do sometimes, but He never stops loving us. When you finally come to understand this awesome truth, it can change everything about how you relate to Him. He's not upset. He doesn't play hard to get, or any games, for that matter.

If you feel like God is mad at you, you've been eating fruit from the wrong tree. You don't need to change to get God to love you. He loves you so that you change. You don't need to get your act together for God to love you; God's love for you is the key to getting your act together.

The order of things is crucial.

1) "But God demonstrates his own love for us in this: While we were still sinners, Christ died for us" (Romans 5:8).

2) "We love Him because He first loved us" (1 John 4:19).

3) Focusing on External Duty vs. Focusing on Internal Desire

Our world emphasizes action. Just do it. Do it now. Do it better. Do more. Even if you don't want to, still do it. And this quickly turns Christian living into something forced and frustrating.

Our world emphasizes duty as well. That's not a bad thing, per se. Things work better when people accept responsibility. A good work ethic is important. But when that starts to inform and define how we approach spiritual things, we are on our way to toxic "religion."

When, however, I look at Christian living as the joy of my life, that's transforming. We take the most important journey of life—from "have to" to "get to". The apostle John put it this way: "In fact, this is love for God: to keep his commands. And his commands are not burdensome," in 1 John 5:3 (NIV).

In other words, if obeying God is becoming a burden to you, love is missing.

You've heard the saying, "No pain; no gain." Well, when it comes to godliness, if there is pain because of your effort, there is no real gain—or growth.

LIVING IN THE RIGHT TREE

It all comes down to eating from the right tree. It determines whether we live in dead religion, a life-giving, abundant relationship with God. I want to share three things that will help you eat the fruit of the tree of life and choose relationship over religion.

1) Fall in Love with Jesus

This may seem to be a no-brainer, something glaringly obvious, but it needs to be front and center in our hearts and minds. We sing about loving Jesus, we talk about loving Jesus, and we know how important it is—in our minds. But what about our hearts? Note the specific language I'm using. I am not saying we need to love Jesus. I'm talking about falling in love with Him. You may see these two things as interchangeable—synonyms—but they are different.

Think about it this way. You love people in your life, from family to friends. But you don't love them in the same way, or with the same intensity, as you love the one with whom you are *in love*. The difference is one of focus and degree. Loving our neighbors, for example (something explicitly commanded by God), means treating them fairly and looking out for their welfare, among other things.

But being *in love* with someone is much more intense. It involves passion and can approach obsession. When you're in love, you're preoccupied. You long for their presence. It's a powerful experience, one that is thrilling and exciting. It can be overwhelming.

How many of us feel that way about Jesus?

Whenever I talk about this, either in personal conversation or when I am teaching, I know someone will ask, "Pastor, you make it sound so easy. But how do you do that? How do you fall in love with Jesus?" My answer usually involves two things that cause me to love him.

When we love Jesus, something inside us desires to do good and treat people right.

The first thing that draws me into an intense love relationship with Jesus is who He is. A healthy and loving relationship with Jesus starts with our image of Him. If you have an image of God as some kind of stone-faced Abraham Lincoln figure who is perpetually disappointed with us, you're going to find it hard to love that false image of God.

But when I have the image of God that lines up with His word, where He smiles and laughs over us and loves us unconditionally (even when we fall short or fail), something happens in our hearts. We find ourselves falling in love with Him every day. Knowing who He is frees us from the falsehood that God is out there somewhere rather than within you. Jesus is the ultimate image of God; through Jesus we have been gifted with the Holy Spirit, and "...where the Spirit of the Lord is, there is freedom" (Micah 3:17).

The second thing that helps us fall in love with Jesus is to focus on what He has done.

His finished work.

This will always draw us in and captivate our hearts. What He did for us was over-the-top—the greatest demonstration of love ever. When we take our eyes off of the distractions of life and this present world and turn our full attention to Jesus and how He has loved us and paid our sin debt, our hearts are awakened and it's like love at first sight—but every hour of every day.

There's a verse that I'm convinced most of us read but don't really connect with: "If you love me, you will obey what I command" (John 14:15). Sadly, too many Christians read that short but power-packed verse through the prism of the wrong tree: "If I behave, treat people right, and do the right thing, then I'm showing I love God." The idea is that love is earned by being good or doing certain things. Conditional love.

But that's not what Jesus is saying.

The key is in the punctuation, that subtle comma—on which side are you?

"If you love me, YOU WILL…"

The correct reading is that when we love Jesus, something inside us desires to do good and treat people right. Not, if you do certain things that means you love Him—but because you love Him you will live different. Reading the verse through the prism of the right tree means you know you're messed up, but that just makes you love Him more.

Let me use marriage as an illustration. It's not like God is saying, "Jason, be faithful to Veronica because there is a command about it. Though shalt not commit adultery." Using King James voice always sounds better.

So, you close your eyes to other women every day. And you try *really* hard not to break the law.

Frankly, if the reason you stay faithful to your spouse is because you should, or because there's a commandment that says you should, you are closer to infidelity than you might think. This kind of thinking is from the wrong tree.

But if you are really *in love* with your spouse, you don't need a rule to remind you. Faithfulness is intuitive and instinctive. Love fuels all things good. That's why there is so much about it in the Bible. I love what Paul wrote to the Galatians: "But the fruit of the Spirit is love, joy, peace, forbearance, kindness, goodness, faithfulness, gentleness, and self-control. Against such things there is no law" (Galatians 5:22-23).

When our hearts are filled with love for Jesus, the fruit comes naturally.

Or should I say, *supernaturally.*

So, fall in love with Jesus.

2) Don't Allow Condemnation to Consume You

The second key to living in the Tree of Life involves a word most of us are all-too-familiar with—*condemnation*. A term tied to the ideas of judgment and punishment. And it is something that most of us struggle with throughout life. But we don't have to. We can find freedom from it through what Jesus has done for us.

Condemnation is toxic. It corrupts our minds and undermines our relationships.

We need to have zero-tolerance for condemnation.

- "Therefore, there is now no condemnation for those who are in Christ Jesus, because through Christ Jesus the law of the Spirit who gives life has set you free from the law of sin and death." (Romans 8:1-2)
- "Who then is the one who condemns? No one. Christ Jesus who died—more than that, who was raised to life—is at the right hand of God and is also interceding for us." (Romans 8:34)

The devil works overtime trying to keep us tied up in condemnation-driven knots. How he dealt with our ancestors in the Garden of Eden is how he deals with us. The basic elements of temptation never change, whether we're talking about forbidden fruit, addiction, ego, or even religion. His goal is to get us involved in something that appeals to our flesh and then add copious amounts of condemnation.

And I'm not just talking about self-condemnation, but others-condemnation as well. Don't allow it! In fact, one of the best ways to see if you're eating from the wrong tree and choosing religion over relationship is how you view other people. If you find yourself being judgmental or hyper-critical, check your tree. When you think about people who don't seem to measure up to your expectations, you are on the wrong side of that comma. Remember—Jesus didn't just liberate you for you; He liberated you to liberate others.

Don't allow condemnation to consume you.

3) Choose the Tree of Life Everyday

There is something about a new day. It brings new opportunities and experiences—some good and some not-so-good. I'd like to be able to tell you that you can choose relationship over religion and never have to face this issue again, but that's not how it works. Just as during their time in the wilderness, the children of Israel had to get up each morning and gather God's miraculous provision of manna, so we have to start each day by choosing to live in the Tree of Life. This is how we experience what the prophet Jeremiah described as the new mercies of God every morning (Lamentations 3:22-23).

You will always experience a pull toward the wrong tree, no matter how long you've been saved or how mature you may think you are in Christ. Within the deceitful heart of mankind is a leaning toward religion—becoming godly or good our own way. So, we must make the choice every day to live grace-centered lives and pursue a personal and passionate relationship with God. This is as important today as it was thousands of years ago when God gave these words to a man called Moses:

> *This day I call the heavens and the earth as witnesses against you that I have set before you life and death, blessings and curses.* **Now choose life**, *so that you and your children may live.*
> —*Deuteronomy 30:19* (**emphasis added**)

Notice that this choice of life, choosing relationship over religion, is tied to a generational blessing to our children. The sad reality is, the choices we make will affect our children, just as the choices of our ancestors have affected us. This is why we need to move to step four in our journey of freedom and break the cycles of generational curses.

BREAKING THE CYCLE OF GENERATIONAL CURSES

Most people don't wake up and say, "I'm going to meet someone and get married today." For most folks, the process of marriage starts with meeting someone. If you like him or her, you'll date a while. If the two of you grow to love one another, then one of you proposes, the other accepts, and a wedding date is set. Each step along the way you learn more about the person. At some point, you begin to evaluate them with an eye toward their suitability as a life partner.

But you need to evaluate yourself, too—perhaps first—to see what you're bringing to the relationship and to your partner. What strengths are you bringing; what are you doing to develop them further? What habits have you established that work toward wholeness in Christ?

And what weaknesses are you bringing with you; what known sin are you hiding—or ignoring? What issues are tagging along behind you? It would behoove you to work those issues out so that you can enter into a relationship as a whole individual in Christ rather than taking old hurt and brokenness with you.

If you're already married, you might be able to identify dysfunctions in how you relate to one another? Know that the seeds of those problems existed in you already, though they may have only manifested after you started the relationship, or even after marriage. You may be thinking, "It's her, not me!", or "Certainly, it's him, not me!". But in reality, you know you've both got skin in this game.

If you're not yet married, this is the best time to deal with our dysfunctions before they become real problems. Marriage is only one example out of hundreds I could use, but the point is that we all have brokenness within us. Some of it comes from us. Some of it comes from others. Some of it simply comes from the sinful nature we've all inherited from Adam and Eve. Brokenness is a given. But sometimes it becomes systemic, a cycle that repeats itself from generation to generation. These cycles can reach far into the past, and you may very likely pass them on to your own children if you don't face them and take steps to break them.

What generational curses do you need to break for your family?

The good news is, curses are not the only things that are passed down—blessings are, too!

GENERATIONAL CURSES AND BLESSINGS

I want to talk about a principle in God's word that is at work inside each and every one of us.

God desires to get things into us, and one of the primary ways he does this is through our relational connections. The Bible talks quite a bit about generational blessings and generational curses.

God is taking something he has, and is putting it in people, and his expectation is that one generation is sharing that to the next generation. And not just in the practical sense, but there is a spiritual dynamic. A spiritual DNA that is being transferred.

Now in order for this transference to take place, God had to take a risk, because the bad gets transferred as well. And we can see that clearly. We see crazy statistics—like 97% of those who abuse children, were abused as children. So the thing they grew up hating the most, they end up doing that. What is that? That's not just a warped mind, there's a spiritual transference that is taking place. But God allows that process to happen because he wanted to put blessings inside of all of us.

The reality is, whatever doesn't get transformed gets transmitted to the next generation

---

Systemic brokenness affects everything in the same way that color-blindness affects everything. You may see just fine, but the colors are off. Of course, colorblindness is not a matter of character—but what if it was? What if, instead of having difficulty seeing the difference between red and green, one had difficulty seeing the difference between "mine" and "yours"? Or the difference between "love" and "weakness"? What if one only saw goodness as an opportunity for exploitation? And what if such moral misperceptions were passed down from parent to child the way colorblindness is? Believe me, they are. And these cycles have been showing up for thousands of years. I call them *generational curses*.

If you don't break them, they will break you.

The reality is, whatever doesn't get transformed gets transmitted to the next generation. Your children will have to confront the sins and strongholds that you were unwilling to defeat. So many of us have predispositions and predilections that are influencing us that we don't even recognize. There are things that are influencing our behaviors and habits that we have likely never seen. They were handed down to us. We grew up in an environment and were taught certain patterns, behaviors, habits, and attitudes. I know Jesus is in your heart, but grandpa is still in your bones. These influencing forces from the past are affecting our life and relationships in the present.

But first, allow me to elaborate. Generational curses are not like voodoo. They're just sins—habits, behaviors, mindsets, and patterns. It's disobedience to God that becomes habitual and familial; it comes from within—not a curse put on you from the outside. Generational curses are handed down to us through the generations, from parents or extended family. Sometimes, they're just a negative tendency, an unhealthy way of thinking, or an attitude that's not beneficial for healthy life and healthy relationships, but they become pervasive.

These principles of generational curses also hold true for generational blessings. Like opposite sides of the same coin, humanity passes its heritage from parent to child for better or worse. Though each individual has a free will to choose, our early choices are dependent on what our families or caretakers offer.

So, there are only two points on the spectrum of generational passing: curses and blessings. Where a family or person falls on this spectrum is what makes each one unique. The closer to one end or the other, the greater the blessing or the curse. And this is not a time when *balance* is the desirable end! Blessing is always the greatest good, but it requires obedience to God; because we're human, curses are the more common heritage.

Your actions, your behaviors, your habits, the sin, the things that you're messing around with, will pass through you and not end with you.

Whatever the prevailing direction of the family, it becomes pervasive, and it's subtle. Children absorb it like air and milk and accept it as normal. Because it is normal, it isn't questioned, it's simply accepted as how life is, what families do, who we are. As a child, how often did you think curse words were the best way to show displeasure? Or how old were you the first time you questioned whether anger and violence *should* come together? Or if silence and avoidance really got the desired results? If you grew up with these behaviors, you may not have liked them, but you accepted them as the norm, and they probably became your go-to behaviors.

For most of us, generational curses were the heritage we received. I am bearing the outcomes and the pain of some people before me who made some bad decisions and committed some actions they shouldn't have. These are generational curses—the negative things that got passed down to me and I may be passing unknowingly to the next generation.

SOME ESSENTIAL THEOLOGY

In Exodus 20:5-6, when God is giving the commandments, He says, "You shall not bow down to them or worship them; for I, the Lord your God am a jealous God...." He's jealous of our relationship, He *will not* share it with idols. He says, "... punishing the children for the sin of the parents to the third and fourth generation to those who hate me, but showing love to a thousand generations of those who love me and keep my commandments."

Now some of you may be reading that and thinking, *That's messed up God; that doesn't seem fair. You're gonna punish that kid for something his dad or great-granddad did, when he didn't do anything wrong?*

There's a lot of misinterpretation of this text. God is not unfair and he's not unjust. What God means here is that there are consequences for your actions and your sins that the third and fourth generations after you will bear the repercussions for. Your actions, your behaviors, your habits, your sin, and the things that you're messing around with won't end with you. You don't want to take this lightly—your choices today will steal from your family's knowledge of God tomorrow—and people are "destroyed from lack of knowledge" (Hosea 4:6). Recall the ending of chapter three. True freedom is found when you know who God is.

You can see the gravity of generational sin all throughout the scriptures—even for those who lived a good and faithful life. Abraham is a great example of someone who passed on generational sin. Genesis 12:13 tells the story of when Abraham and Sarah, his wife, are going into the land of Egypt. Abraham has already received the promise from God that he's going to be a blessing and produce children, and God's going to protect him and be with him. But he heads into Egypt, afraid that Pharoah would kill him in order to take Sarah as his own wife because of her beauty. So, he begins to doubt that God can protect him there. Abraham didn't trust the promise of God and took matters into his own hands.

He convinces Sarah to play along with him, and they lie to Pharaoh, convincing him that Sarah is Abraham's sister—not his wife.

But the lie doesn't work. If Sarah is only the sister, then to Pharaoh, she was fair game. So, it backfired on him. Pharaoh takes her into his house. But God was still faithful even though Abraham doubted. Disease spreads throughout Pharaoh's house and God reveals to him that this is because he took Abraham's wife. So Pharaoh asks Abraham, "Why did you lie to me? You brought a curse onto me because of this woman. Take her and go" (Genesis 12: 18-19, author paraphrase).

What Abe may have thought was just a little white lie grew into a generational lying spirit. We know that is so because in Genesis 26, his son Isaac, the child of promise, follows his father's example, even though he hadn't himself witnessed the white lie. A lying spirit was part of his environment, a legacy from his father.

In Genesis 26, Isaac is living in a foreign land, and he gets the same promise from God to live as a foreigner in the land, and that God would be with him as his covering and protection just like He was with his father, Abraham. So, Isaac stayed in the land of Guar. And when the men who lived there asked Isaac about his wife Rebecca, he lied—the same lie that Abraham told. After all, this is what daddy did when he was in trouble.

And you see this lying spirit grow even more to the next generation. In Genesis 27, Isaac had two sons, Esau and Jacob, and it was time for Esau, the eldest, to get his blessing from his aging and nearly blind father. But Isaac's wife, Rebecca, wants the blessing to go to Jacob, so she tells Jacob to act like Esau by talking like him and taking him his favorite stew. But Jacob is scared. He tells his mom, "Esau's so hairy and I'm not. What if my father touches me and he realizes that I'm trying to trick him? He'll curse me instead of bless me. (v. 11-12)" She responds, "We'll put fur on your hands and arms, and he'll be convinced." So he eagerly agrees to deceive his father and steal his brother's blessing (which was all that Esau had left because he'd traded his birthright to Jacob for some food, long before).

What I want you to pay special attention to is that when generational sin isn't dealt with, it multiplies the stronghold for the next generation.

Abraham, Isaac, Jacob—the patriarchs of God's Chosen People— passed on both blessing and curses. King David, whom God called the man after His own heart, passed on some generational curses to his children as his legacy. One of them was lust. He was a lustful man.

He took many wives and concubines when he wasn't supposed to. He brought Bathsheba into his house and had sex with her even though she was a married woman.

And, yes, he repented and God was gracious and merciful to him (and will always be gracious and merciful to those of us who turn and repent), but David didn't deal with it fully because you see it passed on to Solomon who had 700 wives and 300 concubines—far more than the number of women David had. And it was through Solomon's wives that pagan worship infiltrated back into Israel. Solomon's heart drifted from God to satisfy his pagan wives, and he eventually worshipped the pagan gods with them. Why? Because of the generational sin that was passed down to him.

We can see this generational transference take place not only in the scriptures, but in modern times as well. In 1874, a member of the New York State prison board noticed that there were five members of the same family in their prison at the same time. The board was shocked. They wondered, *what happened to this family?* So, they did some research to find the genesis of the depravity.

They traced it all the way back to an ancestor born in 1720.

The man was known for being a lazy guy, a troublemaker, someone of low moral character, and an alcoholic. But, to make matters worse, he married a woman who was just like him: low moral character, an alcoholic, and a troublemaker.

They had six daughters and two sons. But by 1874, this troublesome couple had approximately 1,200 descendants.

Here's what they learned about them:

- 310 were *homeless*.
- 160 were *prostitutes*.
- 180 suffered from *drug or alcohol abuse*.

- 150 were *criminals* who spent time in prison.
- 7 were *murderers*.

This is the power of only one couple, and an example of the harmful dysfunction that can be passed down from one generation to the next.

In contrast, they also studied a couple from around the same time. Jonathan Edwards, born in 1703, was a preacher and a deeply spiritual man. He married a woman named Sarah Deeply, a spiritual woman who shared the same values. They were very, very poor, from impoverished families, but he was a dedicated family man. They had eleven children together. At the time of the study in 1874, this couple had 1,400 descendants.

Here's what they found:

- Jonathan Edwards eventually became the *President of Princeton University*.
- 13 of his children were *college presidents*.
- 65 were *college professors*.
- 100 were *attorneys*.
- 32 were *state judges*.
- 85 were *authors* of classic books.
- 66 were *physicians*.
- 80 held *political offices*, including 3 *state governors* and 3 *senators*.
- 1 became the *Vice President of the United States*.

Your life can either be a stepping stone for your family to go higher or a stumbling block that causes them to struggle.

This is a prime example of generational blessings. We have been given both generational blessings *and* generational curses. And we are passing both on to our children and their children.

Your life can either be a stepping stone for your family to go higher or a stumbling block that causes them to struggle. And here's why: some of you are living for the weekend, and some of you are living for next month. Stop living so shortsighted; live generationally. We serve a generational God. He is the God of Abraham, Isaac, and Jacob.

And he is not just interested in your life. He's interested in your descendants. He's interested in a godly legacy. Malachi 2:15 says, "Has not the one God made you? You belong to him in body and spirit. And what does the one God seek? Godly *offspring*".

What God wants is a family.

Generations.

A legacy.

While Abraham and David were examples of the passing of generational curses, they are even better examples for passing generational blessings.

God called Abraham out of his father's house, where they had a pagan culture, to follow the one true God wholeheartedly.

And because he would be called the father of the faithful and because of his devotion to God, God made some promises to him. He said in Genesis 12:2-3:

> *I will make you into a great nation, and I will bless you; I will make your name great, and you will be a blessing. I will bless those who bless you, and whoever curses you I will curse; and all peoples on earth will be blessed through you.*

In Genesis 13:16, God makes a promise to Abraham because of his faithfulness in following God. He says, "I'll make your offspring like the dust of the earth so that if anyone could count the dust, then your offspring could be counted." So, the promise wasn't even so much for him. He wasn't going to see more than the merest beginning of the promise of God. His grandsons, Esau and Jacob, were only fifteen years old when Abraham died. The fulfillment of that promise was for his descendants. And 2,000 years later, out of Abraham's descendants would come Jesus Christ, who would bear the sins of all mankind and offer eternal life in heaven. That was the generational blessing that he passed on.

Hundreds of years after David died, Luke writes in Acts 13:22-23, "God testified concerning him, I have found David, son of Jesse, a man after my own heart; he'll do everything I want him to do." From David's descendants, God brought to Israel the Savior, Jesus, as He promised. So, David was a descendant of Abraham but also one of the great-grandfathers of Jesus Christ. Later, God would go on to bless Abijah, David's great-grandson. (See 1 Kings 15.)

Do you see what a powerful influence just one individual can have on generations after them? Do you realize that you can be that Abraham, you can be that David, impacting generations after you, that the curse and consequence that you inherited doesn't have to flow through you to the next generation? The reality is, we are all a product of our heritage.

But we must recognize it and make the decision that generational cursrs are going to stop with us. God actually gives you this choice. You don't have to follow the pattern. Here's a choice that God gave to Israelites that He is giving you today:

This day I call the heavens and the earth as witnesses against you that I have set before you life and death, blessings and curses. Now choose life, so that you and your children may live and that you may love the Lord your God, listen to his voice, and hold fast to him. —*Deuteronomy 30:19*

God says, "I'm setting before you a choice. You can choose the curse that you inherited or the blessing that I've given you." And then He says, "Let me give you the right answer: Choose life."

I hope that you stop living your life as if it's only your life. If you can live this life with future generations in mind, then you're going to steward it accordingly.

I believe you can break the cycles of generational consequences and sins that have been passed on to you.

But how?

CALL IT OUT

Number one, you've got to call that thing out. Call out the sin—the habit—the pattern. Stop getting comfortable with it. Declare out loud "I'm done with that."

If you're dealing with an issue or family history, you've got to confront those problems. Sometimes you will hear people say, "Oh, it just runs in the family." "We're just like that." "We're just drinkers in this family." "We're just angry people in this family." When you hear someone say this, tell them, "It may have run in the family, but this is where it runs out!" You know why? Because God has given you something different than your DNA.

He's given you *His* DNA. He's given you the Holy Spirit so you can produce a new fruit. You don't have to produce the fruit of your fathers.

You can produce the fruit of your Heavenly Father. Ephesians 4 (author paraphrase) says you were taught to put that stuff off, put off the old soft self, put off the old habits, put off that old dysfunction—put it all off. It's all been corrupted by deceitful desires and is to be made new in the attitude of your minds.

Now if you really want to call that thing out, but some of it is hidden, here's a secret method to identify those: Give the people around you the permission to tell you when something you're doing is hurting them, *without being defensive or dismissive.*

Because what those dysfunctions passed down to us are doing is hurting the people around you. Just give the people around you permission—"Hey, it's okay. I'm not gonna bite your head off. I'm not gonna yell at you. I'm not gonna be dismissive. I wanna break them." If you can do that, you can identify the generational things that you got comfortable with and no longer see, or never saw at all.

STEP OUT

Second, you've got to step out from among them.

When God calls you, he calls you to step out. He called Abraham to step out of Harran, out of the sins of his fathers and the pagan culture. When you call that thing out, you've got to step out from among the people who are causing the dysfunction. I'm not advocating that kids should run away from home and spouses should divorce each other. But I am saying that there are some dysfunctions that are so bad, they are leading toward a path of generational death. Here's what Paul says in 2 Corinthians 6:17 about being unequally yoked. He says, "Come out from them and be separate, says the Lord."

The places where you open your heart need to be among those who seek the Lord.

I'm not saying avoid non-Christians, but to live your life differently than them. You've got to get around people who have the same morals, same values, and who are going the same direction. Jesus spent much of His time among unbelievers, but He spent His private time among His 12 disciples, His most private time with only three of them, and His very most private time alone with the Father. The places where you open your heart need to be among those who seek the Lord.

It's quite possible some of those people you need to come out of could share your last name.

I remember waking up one morning when I was in fourth grade. I was scared. I was depressed. I got dressed so slowly because I was afraid that my family was going to forget my birthday—again. They forgot it the previous year. I grew up in a family with no dad. My mom didn't even really want to be a parent. So we didn't celebrate stuff like that. We weren't celebrated. But that was in third grade, and it was hurtful to me.

So, a year went by, and I woke up that day afraid of what would happen. And the whole time I was walking with my brothers to school, I was thinking, "I wonder if they're gonna say anything." But I didn't say anything. I didn't say, "Hey, it's my birthday, guys." I think I was sitting in my self-pity but also testing them. But they didn't say anything. So, I got to school and my best friend, Mikey, came right over to me and gave me a hug and said, "Happy birthday, dude." And he asked, "What are you gonna do today?"

And I said, "I don't know. You know, they didn't say anything." He was one of the few people in my life that knew they forgot last year. So, he just broke the awkwardness. He said, "Well, I'm sure they'll do something, man." And we just went about the day. So after school, I took extra time playing with my friends because I was afraid to go home, so I stalled.

Then, my buddy, Mikey, had to go. He ran off, but I still stalled. One by one, everyone headed home until it was just me. With resistance, I slowly walked home. I got within a few houses of my home and saw all my brothers coming out of the house, running to the car. My mom came out yelling at them. I hurried up, thinking we were going somewhere, and she saw me coming.

She said, "Where the heck were you? We've been waiting for you so long. We're gonna go out to eat."

I said, "Well, I'm here now. I'm sorry."

She said, "No, you're not going with us. You get inside that house."

I begged her to change her mind.

"Nope, get inside that house." She added some more explicit words that I won't type out. I could've put up a fight, but I didn't. I was already feeling pitiful. So, I went into the house and cried. They left and I just sat there in my tears, feeling bad for myself.

Shortly after, the phone rang. It was my buddy, Mikey, who lived just a block and a half away. And he said, "Hey, man, what are you doing? Can I come over for your birthday? What's happening?"

I said, "No, they forgot."

"Oh man. I'm so sorry. Do you wanna come over?" he asked.

I hung up the phone and shuffled over to his house just down the street.

Mikey was there in the front yard to greet me. "Yay! Jason, Happy birthday, man! "Come on in." I came inside the house and his mom was there holding a cake. His dad and his brother were there, too, and they sang me happy birthday. And, after the song, his mom held out a wrapped present.

My buddy, Mikey, left early from playing to race home and tell his mom that it was my birthday, and they needed to do something for me.

Mike's mom pulled out this present and said, "Jason, I'm proud of you. You're a good kid." That was the first time in my life that I ever heard those words spoken to me. It was at that moment that I realized I came from a very dysfunctional, abusive family. When I talk about abuse, I mean bloody abuse. Like broken jaws, throwing knives and forks, and other harmful objects. And it was at that moment that I saw this healthy family and said to myself, "I don't want an unhealthy family."

I made the decision to step out. I didn't run away, but I realized that my family was harmful, hurtful, toxic, and unhealthy. And I decided to spend as much time as I could with my healthy friends. And while my brothers were getting stitches and bruises and beatings, I grew up among healthier people. God has had His hand on me.

Sometimes what you thought was isolation and opposition was actually God preparing you for an amazing destiny.

You've got to step out. Sometimes you step out, and sometimes God steps you out and you think, *oh, that was punishment.* But it was actually God's protection.

Joseph was sold into slavery. It felt like punishment. But here he was in a dysfunctional family, and God was insistent on pulling Joseph away from them and using it to teach him and bless him.

And when David was young, forgotten in the field, God said, "I've got to separate David. I don't want him with his dad and his brothers. I need him to be different."

Sometimes what you thought was isolation and opposition was actually God preparing you for an amazing destiny.

So, the road to true freedom is not only found in what you pursue and allow into your life; it is also found in the departure from those things that are keeping you from it.

SEEK OUT HELP AND HEALING

Number three, you need to seek out help and healing. You men, especially.

This is one of the hardest places to get to because we like to think or project that we've got it all together. We'd rather isolate and try to self-heal or deal with it alone. Whether because of our own choices or the choices of people before us, we need to seek out help in healing.

We are human. We all have some habits that were passed down to us that we need help with, either from a pastor, a coach, a small group, a team—whoever it may be, you need to get around people who will partner with God so that they can partner with you.

James 5:16 says this, "Therefore confess your sins to each other and pray for each other so that you may be healed." This is the reason why you need to seek out help and healing, because God actually has healing for you but it's not going to come when you seek it in yourself, by yourself. If you want to break the generational curses in Jesus's name and multiply generational blessings, you've got to call it out, step out, and seek out.

LIVE IT OUT

Finally, you have to live out your new identity in Christ. Thank God that He has broken the curse. Do you know that there is now a new inheritance? You are grafted into the family of God. The Bible says you've been adopted into this family, sewn into every inheritance of Abraham, Isaac, and Jacob, and every blessing that was attributed to those are attributed now to you in Christ.

Here's what Romans 5:12 says, "Therefore, just as sin entered the world through one man . . . " this is the generational sin—the sin of one man and one woman. It didn't stay with Adam. Death multiplied throughout the generations because of one man's sin. ". . . through the disobedience of the one man, the many were made sinners, so also through the obedience of the one man, the many will be made righteous" (Romans 5:19). Because of Jesus, we have a new inheritance, we have a new spirit, we have access to a new DNA and bear new fruit in our lives!

God is saying the same to you: You can start a new pattern of generational blessings for your family.

As mentioned earlier, we see Jacob's lying spirit multiplied in Genesis 32. There, we see the account of when he's wrestling with the angel of the Lord. And in the middle of this wrestling match, the angel asked him, "What is your name?" And in shock, he whispers, "Jacob." I love how the AMP mentions the meaning of the name: "My name is Jacob, supplanter, schemer, trickster. That's who I am."

Now, God did not ask him what his name was because He didn't know. God, the Angel of the Lord, knew his name. He wanted Jacob to see who He was. God said, "Your name will no longer be Jacob, but Israel, because you have struggled with God and with humans and have overcome."

So, God was telling Jacob that even though He never intended him to copy his daddy and grandaddy, He was going to bless him simply because He loved them. God wanted Jacob to be like Him and NOT follow in the footsteps of his ancestors.

God is saying the same to you: You can start a new pattern of generational blessings for your family. You can break the generational curses in Jesus' name. Here's the promise you God gives us to break every curse in Galatians 3:13-14 (TLB):

"But Christ has bought us out from under the doom of that impossible system by taking the curse for our wrongdoing upon himself. For it is written in the Scripture, "Anyone who is hanged on a tree is cursed" (as Jesus was hung upon a wooden cross). Now God can bless the Gentiles, too, with this same blessing he promised to Abraham; and all of us as Christians can have the promised Holy Spirit through this faith."

Once we break the cycles of generational curses, we must learn to hear the voice of the Holy Spirit leading us out into a new destiny. Let's continue the journey in the next chapter, Step Five, Hearing God's Voice.

STEP 5

HEARING GOD'S VOICE

God is speaking. He is a communicating God. He is a God who likes and desires to speak into your life. There is a certain persuasion of thought and theology that says that after the apostles died, God stopped speaking. I want you to know that is not the truth. God still speaks. He desires to communicate to you. If God doesn't speak today, then we do a great disservice to other people by telling them they can have a personal relationship with God. You need to know that God desires to speak to you, and He has always planned to have this intimate relationship with you. Exodus 20:18-19 (NKJV) says:

> *Now all the people witnessed the thunderings, the lightning flashes, the sound of the trumpet, and the mountain smoking; and when the people saw it, they trembled and stood afar off. Then they said to Moses, 'You speak with us, and we will hear; but let not God speak with us, lest we die.'"*

Moses had received the Ten Commandments on Mount Sinai from God. The people, fearful of God's presence, stayed at a distance. And this is what so many people do—even in the body of Christ. Out of shame or fear of what God will do, they stay at a distance from God instead of drawing near to His presence. The Israelites said they would listen to Moses but wouldn't let God speak to them for fear they would die. In this scene, people chose rules over relationship. It seemed less scary to just have Moses tell them the rules—what to do and what not to do. However, it was always God's design and intention to have relationship with us, but instead, the Israelites decided they wanted distance.

Sometimes, it seems easier to get the list of rules and boundaries rather than to engage in relationship. We just want a to-do list. But God wants to speak to us and have a relationship with us. Think about it this way: One person has no social media accounts, and if asked, they will tell you that God told them to get rid of social media. Another person has a popular social media account in which they spread the gospel because God told them to. So, which is the right rule? Is social media inherently bad, or is it an evangelistic tool? The first person has not wrongly stated that God told them to get rid of social media, and the second person is not sinning by posting on social media. See, it's not a hard rule. God wants your relationship. Maybe that means getting rid of social media, or maybe it means creating a social media account to evangelize. Or perhaps, in one season, a person has felt called to give everything away. They are giving more than they ever have. Maybe they are paying for the person behind them in the drive-thru or selflessly sacrificing themselves for others. In the same way, another person may be starting a savings account to be frugal and honor God through good financial stewardship. Both people are being obedient.

For some people, this is frustrating. They want a hard and fast rule from God, but they are sadly missing the point. The point isn't the rules. It's the relationship. Now, obedience to God is very important, and I don't want to understate that. However, you were not meant to meticulously follow rules with a hardened heart, distanced from God. Listen to God's voice. What is He calling you to do? What is He whispering to you? It seems easier to follow a list of rules, but that is not what your connection to God was meant to be. It was meant to be a relationship. We can get so preoccupied with rules and religion that we miss the relationship.

Jesus said that our relationship with Him would be like that of a shepherd and sheep. John 10:3-5 says:

> *The gatekeeper opens the gate for him, and the sheep listen to his voice. He calls his own sheep by name and leads them out. When he has brought out all his own, he goes on ahead of them, and his sheep follow him because they know his voice. But they will never follow a stranger; in fact, they will run away from him because they do not recognize a stranger's voice.*

Jesus's sheep know His voice, and He calls them by name. The sheep, so trusting of Jesus's voice, will never follow the voice of a stranger but rather flee from him because they do not recognize the voice. The sheep are so familiar with the voice of their shepherd that another voice cannot entice them.

There have been so many pivotal moments in my life where I just knew that I was hearing God's voice. For example, I know without any doubt that God told me to marry my wife, Veronica. There has never been a question about whether God told me that she was my wife. God told me to join the Navy. I didn't want to join, but God told me I had deeply engrained issues that needed to be worked out through military discipline. I'm so glad that I knew God's voice and that His voice in my life was louder than my own feelings or desires. When I was going to school to be a physician's assistant, God called me into vocational pastoral ministry. Now, it's worth noting that your workplace is your ministry. However, I knew I was hiding from my calling when I was in school, and God called me to focus fully on the advancement of His Kingdom through His Church. There was even a moment when I heard God ask me, "Are you Mine?" I cannot say that I belong to God if I willingly ignore His call.

God doesn't have a speaking problem. We have a hearing problem.

Many people know the story of how our church, Discovery, came to be—that it started with following God's voice. Years ago, I was driving and frustrated by the traffic. As the frustration was bubbling inside of me, God said to me, "You're going to pastor some of these people who are caught in traffic with you." God still speaks, and He speaks clearly. He is not a God of confusion. Too often though, His words fall on deaf ears.

WEAPONS OF MASS DISTRACTION

Maybe you feel like you don't hear God's voice often. It may seem as though the volume is off, or something is disrupting the frequency. I want to help you identify why you may not be hearing His voice. God is definitely speaking, but for some reason, we are not listening. Let me say it this way. God doesn't have a speaking problem. We have a hearing problem. There are reasons why others appear to have a more personal and intimate relationship with God than you do. There are what I call weapons of mass distraction that the enemy has used to keep us from the purposes, will, and voice of God.

Busyness

The first weapon of mass distraction is busyness. We are just so chronically busy. There is always something to do, the schedule is always full, your mind is always racing. It is difficult to build a relationship with anybody when you are that busy. You have to take time and separate yourself and rest. We have tragically made busyness a norm in our society, and it is drowning out the voice of God in our lives. We can become so focused on tasks and schedules that we forget the most important relationship we have—our relationship with God.

Stop focusing on the provision and fix your focus on the Provider.

Psalm 127:2 (NKJV) says, "It is vain for you to rise up early, to sit up late, to eat the bread of sorrows; For so He gives His beloved sleep." God will take care of your needs. You can trust Him. Stop focusing on the provision you need and focus on the Provider.

Competing Voices

The second weapon of mass distraction is competing voices. In other words, God could be yelling at you, but you have a hundred other things yelling at you, so you cannot distinguish between those voices and the Shepherd's voice. At a sporting event, when the crowd is going wild, you cannot hear the person sitting two seats away from you. Even if they are speaking directly to you, you may not hear them or realize they are talking to you, and you may have to lean in closer and work a lot harder to tune out the other voices to make out what the person is saying. What's incredible, though, is that due to the bowl-like structure of a football stadium, you can carry a conversation with someone on the other side speaking at a normal volume when no one else is there. This is because there are no competing voices. Luke 14:18-20 says:

> *But they all alike began to make excuses. The first said, 'I have just bought a field, and I must go and see it. Please excuse me.' Another said, 'I have just bought five yoke of oxen, and I'm on my way to try them out. Please excuse me.' Still another said, 'I just got married, so I can't come.'"*

These people were not focused on terrible things, but they were focused on the wrong things. They prioritized property, careers, and marriage over the Kingdom of God. Nothing should take priority over God. There will always be an excuse if you look for one.

Is your heart prepared and ready to meet with God or are you just checking off a box?

But what if you were to pause and identify the competing voices against God and take steps to eliminate them? Maybe they can't all be entirely eliminated but can at least be minimized. Maybe you can't throw your phone away, but you can restrict your use of it. You can refrain from spending four hours on social media every day. If you have four extra hours to spend on Instagram, surely you have time to spend with God.

An Unprepared Heart

The third weapon of mass distraction is an unprepared heart. You might go to church on Sundays. Perhaps you open your Bible daily and pray nightly. However, is your heart prepared and ready to meet with God or are you just checking off a box? Bring distractions to God, and deal with them right away so that you will be able to fully absorb what God is saying. Matthew 13:8-9 says, "Still other seed fell on good soil, where it produced a crop—a hundred, sixty, or thirty times what was sown." Prepare your heart that you may be like the good soil who receives the Word of God.

If you truly want to learn to hear and identify God's voice, you must eliminate these weapons of mass distractions. The busyness, the competing voices, and the unprepared heart are intended to prevent you from recognizing God's voice. 2 Corinthians 7:1 says, "Therefore, since we have these promises, dear friends, let us purify ourselves from everything that contaminates body and spirit, perfecting holiness out of reverence for God." Purify yourself from every distraction. Do whatever you have to do to eliminate your distractions. Set time limits on your phone, delete your social media, wake up earlier, and limit anything that could hinder your relationship with God.

GETTING ON THE FREQUENCY OF HEAVEN

There is a powerful illustration that can help you understand the frequency of Heaven. Google a video of a 17.4-kilohertz soundwave known as the mosquito sound. Do you hear the sound? If you are younger, you might be able to. If you are older, you may be unable to hear it. They say that when people reach around the age of forty, enough damage to the ear has occurred that they can no longer hear the sound. This sound is almost painful for some people, yet others can't even hear it. Regardless of whether you can hear that frequency or not, the sound is very real and present. Similarly, God is speaking, but do you hear Him? Are you listening? The inability to hear the mosquito sound is due to the damage that comes with age, but our inability to hear God's voice is due to the damage from tuning Him out, allowing competing voices and busyness to distract us, or having an unprepared heart. Funny enough, Jesus says that unless you become like a little child, you cannot enter the Kingdom of God. The wonderful news, though, is that no matter the damage that has been done, your ability to hear God's voice can be restored. You can return to that childlike state. You can tune your heart back to God's frequency.

Let's take a look at a time in the scriptures when God spoke to a young boy named Samuel. I'm going to point out a few things while you read through this story. In 1 Samuel 3:1-11 (author commentary inserted) says:

The boy Samuel ministered before the Lord under Eli. In those days the word of the Lord was rare; (the truth is that God was still speaking; they just weren't hearing Him) *there were not many visions.* (They weren't dreaming anymore.) *One night Eli, whose eyes were becoming so weak that he could barely see, was lying down in his usual place. The lamp of God had not yet gone out, and Samuel was lying down in the house of the Lord, where the ark of God was. Then the Lord called Samuel. Samuel answered, 'Here I am.' And he ran to Eli and said, 'Here I am; you called me.' But Eli said, 'I did not call; go back and lie down.' So he went and lay down. Again the Lord called, 'Samuel!' And Samuel got up and went to Eli and said, 'Here I am; you called me.' 'My son,' Eli said, 'I did not call; go back and lie down. Now Samuel did not yet know the Lord: The word of the Lord had not yet been revealed to him.* (So, he was hearing God, but he didn't know what to do with it yet). *A third time the Lord called, 'Samuel!' And Samuel got up and went to Eli and said, 'Here I am; you called me.' Then Eli realized that the Lord was calling the boy. So Eli told Samuel, 'Go and lie down, and if he calls you, say,* (this is what I want you to say to God every day) *"Speak, Lord, for your servant is listening."' So Samuel went and lay down in his place. The Lord came and stood there, calling as at the other times, 'Samuel! Samuel!' Then Samuel said, 'Speak, for your servant is listening.' And the Lord said to Samuel: 'See, I am about to do something in Israel that will make the ears of everyone who hears about it tingle.'"*

Samuel was hearing God's voice but was not accustomed to hearing Him. Let me give you some practical steps as you walk out your freedom journey how you tune in to the voice of God in your life.

Set an Appointment

You must set an appointment. We make time for what we value, so schedule it. You set appointments with your doctor and your kid's teachers; you set appointments for meetings and people you may not even really want to meet with. Yet, we fail to set appointments with God. Exodus 19:10-11 (NKJV) says, "Then the LORD said to Moses, 'Go to the people and consecrate them today and tomorrow, and let them wash their clothes. And let them be ready for the third day. For on the third day the Lord will come down upon Mount Sinai in the sight of all the people.'" Setting an appointed time to spend with God is a great idea. You make time for other things, and you schedule those things. When and where are you going to meet with God? I meet with

God in the mornings. I don't do anything—I don't touch my phone, I don't work out, I don't meet with anyone—until I have spent time with God. God is my priority. Nothing else matters if I don't have God.

The quieter you become, the more you can hear.

Be Still and Worship

Be still and worship. Psalm 46:10 (NKJV) says, "Be still, and know that I am God . . ." The quieter you become, the more you can hear. 2 Chronicles 20:17 (NKJV) says, "'You will not need to fight in this battle. Position yourselves, stand still and see the salvation of the LORD, who is with you, O Judah and Jerusalem!' Do not fear or be dismayed; tomorrow go out against them, for the LORD is with you.'" Position yourselves by getting in the Word, soaking in the presence of God, and being in the body. Stillness and worship are difficult for a lot of people. We allow our minds to race. We struggle to sit still. Trust God to fight your battles, and be still. Some people have a better relationship with their Bible than with God. Please, don't take this the wrong way—I am not suggesting that you should read your Bible less. There are people who know the Bible very well, but they don't know God. They can quote scripture, but they can't tell you about God's heart. Be still. Worship. Listen. Know God's heart.

Pray and Read

Pray and read. Get into God's Word. Talk to Him. Tell Him your needs. Get in a solitary place, away from competing voices and distractions. Psalm 119:147 (NKJV) says, "I rise before the dawning of the morning, and cry for help; I hope in Your word." Go to Him first. Pray for whatever is on your heart. If your marriage is on your heart, pray about it. If your career, finances, children, friends, etc. is on your heart, pray about it. Open your Bible and read. Take in the Word of God. Sew it into your spirit. The point of reading is not to check off a box but to hear His voice and know His Word.

Listen and Write

Listen and write. Write as you study and pray. Write what you hear God saying. Value His voice. The more you do this, the more you'll recognize His voice. Habakkuk 2:2 (NKJV) says, "Then the Lord answered me and said: 'Write the vision And make it plain on tablets, That he may run who reads it.'" Schedule time with God. Be still and worship. Pray and read His Word. Listen and write what He says.

THE STRANGERS VOICE

Have you ever seen a video of a huge gathering of sheep with different shepherds? Sheep follow their noses when they graze, so a group of several flocks can be completely intermingled in a field. But when the shepherds call to their flocks, each individual sheep makes a beeline to its own shepherd, and those whose shepherd has not called pay no attention at all and continue to graze. It's like watching an anthill sort itself.

"But they will never follow a stranger; in fact, they will run away from him because they do not recognize a stranger's voice" (John 10:5). The devil actually has a voice, too, and he likes to talk. The Bible tells us in 2 Corinthians 11:14 that he even "masquerades as an angel of light." So, how do we recognize when it's God's voice speaking to us? How do I know it's not an "angel of light", or just me? Could it be my own wishful thinking, my own soul, my own emotions?

I don't know if you've ever been in a situation where someone has given you a "word" because she felt led by the Holy Spirit. We often call that a prophetic word. It's one of the gifts of the Holy Spirit and an operation of the Holy Spirit—it's very real. Throughout my faith journey, I've been really fortunate to have prophetic words spoken into my life by mature spiritual leaders. They were very encouraging, life-giving words. But they haven't always been life-giving. Sometimes I got some words that made me think, *Come on, man, that was not God.*

Maybe this scenario has happened to you or someone you know. A person might say something like this: "I've got a word from God". And then they put their hand on you, and the "word" was just so off. It's happened to me too. I'd say, "Okay," and just let him go. But afterward, I'd say, "Hey, thank you so much, but you missed God on that one." We all miss the mark sometimes. Some people say, "Well, that stuff should never happen in church." But honestly, it kind of has to happen. Because if we're all going to posture ourselves to hear God speak to us, and we want to respond to His voice, then like children, we have to make mistakes to learn that skill. None of us are perfect. We're going to miss it and get it wrong sometimes.

Think of Simon Peter. In Matthew chapter 16, Jesus asked the whole group of His disciples, "Who do you say that I am?" Simon stood up and said, "You are the Messiah, the Son of the living God." And Jesus looked at him and said, "Whoa, Simon, there's no way you could have known that unless God revealed that to you. God spoke to you, Simon." And Jesus gave him a new name: Peter, which means "the rock". And then only moments later, Jesus starts talking about his death. Peter rises up and denies that this will ever happen, and Jesus turns and says, "Get behind me, Satan!" From one moment to the next, Peter went from hearing from heaven to literally hearing from hell.

So, what do we do about that? There needs to be a test. And John addresses that in 1 John 4:1, "Dear friends, do not believe every spirit, but test the spirits to see whether they are from God, because many false prophets have gone out into the world." Don't just believe every prompting, every idea, every compelling "word". Don't believe every spirit, but test—notice the plural here—the spirits. The Holy Spirit will not be offended if you test what you hear from Him.

Not too long ago, a guy came to me and literally said, "I feel like God is leading me to leave my wife and marry my mistress. I feel like I'm supposed to be with this person." And inside I'm thinking, *You have got to be kidding me.* Have you ever seen the Batman and Robin meme where Batman just smacks the crud outta Robin? I felt like reenacting that. This guy did not know the true character of God. He was confused—even worse, He was blind to His own confusion—and that's what the lure of the flesh does. It keeps you enslaved to your flesh *and* deceives you into believing that the pull of your flesh is the pull of God!

God doesn't just want you happy. He wants you holy.

Proverbs 14:12 says, "There is a way that appears right, but in the end it leads to death." It feels right, looks right, seems good, but it isn't. There is no verse in the entire Bible that says that God wants you happy. No, God doesn't just want you happy. He wants you holy. So, there is a way that appears to be right, but in the end, it'll kill you. It leads to death.

If you want greater confidence that you are hearing the voice of God, walk yourself through this four-question test. It will help you walk in the Spirit, *and where the spirit of the Lord is, there is freedom* (2 Corinthians 3:17).

DOES IT LINE UP WITH THE BIBLE?

This is the foundation for discerning who you are hearing from: does the word line up with THE WORD? God's voice will never contradict God's word; He will never tell you to do something that contradicts what He has already written. For example, 1 Corinthians 14 talks about the gift of prophecy. And the Bible is clear that the gift of prophecy is given to strengthen, encourage, and comfort. Any "prophetic" word that brings condemnation is not from God. God's word says that there is no condemnation for those who are in Christ Jesus. So, if you hear a word, filter it through the Bible.

In Matthew 19:3, the Pharisees came and tried to "gotcha" Jesus. They did this often, but on this day, they asked him, "Is it lawful for a man to divorce his wife for any and every reason?" Jesus didn't even answer the question. In verse 4, He simply responded with, "Haven't you read?" and He began to quote Genesis in the Bible. He's saying: "Why do you want my opinion when it's already been written?"

People come up to me often and ask me questions like, "What do you believe about _____, Pastor Jason?" A lot of times it's younger people, because twenty to thirty years ago, we used to call things sin that we don't call sin anymore, and it causes a lot of confusion. So I get these questions, and my answer is the same one that Jesus gave: "What does my opinion on the matter have to do with anything? God's already said, 'It is written. . . .' My opinion on the matter has no bearing." I just point people back to the Bible.

By the way, that's what makes Him God. He has the right to say what is wrong and what is right because he's God. I'm not God. You're not God. Jesus was the one person who was qualified to give His opinion— He was and is God, after all. But He had already given it. Look at what Jesus said in Luke 21: 33, "Heaven and earth will pass away, but my words will never pass away."

What passes for truth may change as culture changes. What used to be called sin may not be called sin anymore by some people. Maybe that thing wasn't actually wrong, then? Or maybe that thing isn't right anymore? Maybe that was just *their* truth? Maybe *my* truth is just different? People say a lot of foolish things, but God's word is forever true. Unchanging. And so, when you're testing the spirit, you need to first ask, "Does it line up with the Bible?"

Now, you've got to be careful. You can't take one verse out of context. Anyone can twist a Bible verse to make it say pretty much whatever they want it to say. In theology, it is called the whole council of God when you view the Bible in its entirety. It is the whole council of God when you take all of the scriptures on a subject, all of what God has to say on that subject, and you bring it together to form your theology and your thoughts. If your interpretation of one section of scripture contradicts another portion of scripture, your interpretation is faulty, and just like my Robin character, you will be imprisoned in confusion.

You don't get your act together then come to Jesus. You come to Jesus so you can get your act together.

Anyone can take a verse and make up their own theology. The devil did that. It is relayed to us in both Matthew 4 and Luke 4. When Jesus was led by the Holy Spirit into the wilderness to be tempted by the devil, the devil showed up at the end of His fasting. The devil quoted the word while trying to tempt the Word of God with the word of God. But Jesus is the living Word of God. Of course, the devil twists scripture, using it out of context. And what does Jesus do? He responds with scripture. "Oh, yeah, devil? It is written. It is written. It is written." So that's the model: check scripture with scripture. Do they agree with each other?

WILL IT MAKE ME MORE LIKE CHRIST?

The second test question is, *will it make me more like Jesus? If I follow through with this thing I'm thinking or feeling I should do, will it make me more like Jesus or less like Jesus?* This is God's goal for every Christian. God's goal for your life is to make you like His Son, to conform you into the image of His Son whom He loves (Romans 8:29). This is God's goal. But don't make this your goal before becoming a Christian. You've got to meet Jesus, fall in love with Jesus and throw open your life to Jesus in order to have the power to live like Jesus. It doesn't work any other way. Let me say it this way: You don't get your act together then come to Jesus. You come to Jesus so you *can* get your act together. Don't get that twisted. Salvation is free. It is not earned. But for everyone who has surrendered their life to God—it is God's goal for your life to make you like Jesus.

Some of you might be unsure how Jesus would act. Let me give you James 3:17-18:

But the wisdom that comes from heaven is first of all pure; then peace-loving, considerate, submissive, full of mercy and good fruit, impartial and sincere. Peacemakers who sow in peace reap a harvest of righteousness.

So, if you want to know if the word you believe is from God, ask, *Is it pure? If I do this, will I be purer? If I send that email, will it be more peace-loving? If I follow through on this prompting, is it considerate? Is it submissive or is it demanding my way? Is it full of mercy or is it full of judgment? Does it bear good fruit: love, joy, peace, patience, kindness, and goodness? Is it impartial? Is it sincere?*

As a pastor, I often give this scripture as advice because I like leading people to Jesus, not leading people to do what I think they should do. I think that's one of my roles as a pastor: to lead you to the one who has all the answers. So often when I give people counsel or advice, I just ask, "What do you think Jesus would do?"

Years ago, a man came to me for counsel. His wife had cheated on him, but in the middle of the restoration process, his friends kept telling him that he should ditch her. They were convinced that she deserved a divorce, and if he stayed, she would just do it again. When he called me, he asked, "Pastor, I'm struggling. What do you think I should do?" And I just said, "I can't tell you what to do, but, what do you think Jesus would do?" And a light bulb went off in his mind. He said, "You know what, Pastor? Jesus has given me so many chances and has been so merciful and loving to me. It's been unfailing. I think I have the faith I need to give her another chance." And I said, "You know what, my friend, I think that sounds a little more like Jesus than the counsel you received from your friends."

And I love what he said next. He said, "You know what, Pastor, I'd rather show up in heaven having given people too much grace than show up in heaven judging people too harshly." See what happened there? This man understood the freedom of God's forgiveness, and this freed him to forgive his wife—and believe me, there is TREMEN-DOUS internal freedom in forgiveness.

I'm not picking on people who have been divorced. I think a lot of churches make divorce their pet sin. But all sin is hateful to God. And Jesus died for all of it. If you're on your second, third, fourth marriage—God loves you. There is restoration and forgiveness. So here's the filter: Is this something that'll make you more like Christ?

Is this question foolproof in isolation? Probably not. But that's why we have the other three tests.

DOES GODLY COUNSEL AGREE?

You've checked the thought against scripture. You've asked yourself if it will make you more like Christ. Now you go to those wise in the ways of the Lord and get counsel from them. That's what the man was doing when his wife was unfaithful. What you're looking for is agreement with godly counsel.

Now let me just insert a disclaimer here, because if you go fishing long enough, you can find *someone* who will give you the answer you want, but you can't just throw the other three questions away and say, "There it is! I got agreement. I'm good to go!" No, you need to use the *whole* test.

If you aren't sure about this particular question, do a little study on 1 Kings 12. It is a true cautionary story on agreement with godly counsel. I'll give you a bird's eye view of it here. Solomon had just died and his son, Rehoboam, was about to be crowned. The kingdom was whole, but

God had told Solomon that it would be split during his son's reign and Jeroboam would take ten of the tribes and reign as king over it, leaving only Judah and Benjamin for Rehoboam. So after King Solomon died, Jeroboam thought, you know what? This is an opportunity. Maybe we can keep the kingdoms of God together and there could be unity. Jeroboam and the rest of Israel came to King Rehoboam, Solomon's son, and said, "Hey, your father forced harsh labor on us; if you lighten the heavy load, we will serve you." So, he had an opportunity to unify the kingdom under his rule. And Rehoboam said, "Go away for three days, and then come back to me for my answer."

King Rehoboam went to the elders who had served King Solomon first. "So, what is your godly counsel?" And the elders said, "If you become a servant to them at this moment in the time of their need, they will serve you as king for the rest of their lives." They gave him this amazing principle of servant leadership. Then, he went to the young men he grew up with for counsel. And their advice was different. They said, "Man, you should tell them, 'You think Solomon was tough and put a harsh yoke on you?' Tell them your yoke's going to be even harder." They said, "Tell them that 'Solomon scourged you with whips; I will scourge you with scorpions.'"

Rehoboam rejected the elder's advice and took the advice that tickled his ears. The ten northern tribes turned their backs on him, and the kingdom of Israel was split from that moment on, all because he didn't get in line with godly counsel. You've got to be careful whom you get your advice from. This takes some discretion. Who can you count on to give you good, godly advice? Your peers are probably not a lot more mature than you are yourself. There are exceptions, of course, and if you have a particularly wise friend, you'll know it. Age doesn't confer wisdom, but more years increase the likelihood of learning wisdom.

Look around you for people who love the Lord, who follow Him, and who know His word and apply it to their own lives. Those are the ones you want to talk to first.

Look at Proverbs 19:20. It says, "Listen to advice," but be willing to "accept discipline," too. That means that you're not going to hear what you think is right sometimes. And you need to be willing to admit, "I missed it, Lord, forgive me." You're probably not going to agree with it all the time, but "at the end you'll be counted among the wise."

Then the next verse in Proverbs 19:21 says, "Many are the plans in a person's heart, but it is the Lord's purpose that prevails." Proverbs 24:6 says, "Surely you need guidance to wage war, and victory is won through many advisers." This is why small groups are so important. You need to be among Christ followers. I'm urging you to get around godly influences and voices bearing the fruit of deep intimacy with God who are speaking into your life.

DO I HAVE PEACE?

I use this one a lot, personally. And I also encourage others often with it. You know what's different about the Christian faith from the others out there? We not only worship God, but our God lives inside of us. So we have the Holy Spirit living inside of us, and we can sense that prompting from Him. Sometimes we even sense the clash between our way and His way—it feels like friction, an inner battle.

The Holy Spirit speaks with peace. Jesus said that it's a peace that the world can't give. There's no pill for it. You won't find it in a relationship. God provides a peace that the world cannot supply. First Corinthians 14:33 (NKJV) says, "For God is not the author of confusion but of peace." That's not God in your confusion because He's the God of Peace.

When we were getting ready to plant Discovery Church, we didn't have the finances to do a lot of things we wanted to do, and there were holdups and difficulties. And one of my spiritual leaders, who was actually a decision-maker with a lot of power, gave me another option. He said, "Well, Jason, I know you've got plans, but there's another church that needs a pastor, and I think you'd do well there." Now, I want you to know, there was not a moment that I thought, "Hmm, let me think about that." I just knew I had peace that God had called me to plant and start Discovery Church. But if I would've done the pros and cons list, one side would show: It's an established church, there's a salary, there's a parsonage, there's *members*. On the other side? Nothing. We were in the red. We've got nobody over here.

What would have appeared to be right would have been the easier choice. But thank God I followed His peace. Now, at the time of writing this book, Discovery is ten years old, and what started with three people has grown to over 3,000 over multiple locations. I followed God's peace. And you can follow that peace, too.

MASTERING YOUR MIND

Here's what I know—You will never change your life until you change the way you think. Our thoughts are powerful, and your life is going to be marked by how well you control your thought life. Your life doesn't begin to change in the doing, it begins to change in the thinking. Romans 12:2 (NLT) says to "let God transform you into a new person by changing the way you think."

When we want to make a change in our lives, we don't usually start with our thinking. This is why our changes don't last long. We will try to change our habits, only to go back after days. We try to stop our addictions, only to fall back into the same patterns we swore we'd never fall back into again. We want to lose weight, so we focus on what we're putting in our mouths, only to fall for the sweet deliciousness of a double-double with animal fries.

You will never change your life until you change the way you think.

This never works because it's not how we change. We have what I call "stinkin thinkin". Walking in freedom is not just found in developing new habits but in escaping old mindsets. It's very likely that your new habits are being thwarted by your old mindsets.

Studies have revealed that the average person has 50,000 thoughts a day, so at this point in our journey together, we have to transform our thinking. We have to train our thoughts in a way that allows us to walk with God and experience change that lasts.

Let's begin by asking the question, "Where does bad thinking come from?"

What's the source?

In previous steps, we've learned about the prison of our past and generational curses. But let's refine our understanding of why we aren't enjoying the freedom we have in Christ by discovering what's really going on in our minds. Because if you don't master your mind, your mind will master you.

WE LET OUR MENTAL SELF-IMAGE DEFINE US

For most of us, our self-image goes way back to our childhood. Unfortunately, some or many of our beliefs are false. Remember as a kid when you would go to a funhouse at a fair and look into those mirrors? They were warped, making you big, skinny, or short. We used to get a kick out of them. They distorted your image.

Some of us grew up around negativity, and we let the words that were spoken over us define us. Unfortunately, many of us have maintained those distorted images of ourselves.

Before David was a king, no one believed in him.

He was #8 in a family of eight.

His dad didn't believe in him. He didn't believe that he could be chosen as the next king of Israel.

Saul didn't think he could fight Goliath.

Goliath was insulted by David as an opponent.

It is no wonder that David wrote in one of the psalms, "But I am a worm and not a man, scorned by everyone and despised by the people" (Psalm 22:6). David had to overcome the negative self-image that he had. He couldn't let it define him. We can't let the way we have come to view ourselves define us. Don't see yourself the way you see yourself. See yourself the way God sees you.

WE LET OUR PAST PROGRAM US

The negative experiences, hurtful words, past mistakes, and the wounds of our past are like a program repeating in our minds.

For some of us, it comes from our family background. You may have had parents who were hard to please. No matter what you did, it was never good enough. Your past has become your programming. Your operating system. David had to get through some bad programming from his past. He wrote in Psalm 13:2, "How long must I wrestle with my thoughts and day after day have sorrow in my heart? How long will my enemy triumph over me?"

I won't go into too much detail about where our thoughts come from because we spent some time on this in a previous chapter. Let me just give you the encouragement of Isaiah 43:18, "Forget the former things; do not dwell on the past."

Unfortunately, we let the world infect us.

The world has a mindset. Media culture is infecting us with their values. We've got Pretty Little Liars showing us how to live, and Victoria bearing all her secrets.

Many of us don't realize how deeply the world is polluting our minds. Scientists have done study after study and have found that you never really forget any scene you see. Even if you don't consciously recall the scene, the image will come right back to your mind if something triggers it. In other words, "garbage in, garbage out". What you put into your mind will inevitably bear fruit in your behavior and beliefs. In fact, when trashy entertainment doesn't bother you anymore, it's a warning light that you've already passed the threshold.

> *Don't become partners with those who reject God. . . . God himself put it this way: 'I'll live in them, move into them; I'll be their God and they'll be my people. So leave the corruption and compromise; leave it for good,' says God. 'Don't link up with those who will pollute you.'* —*2 Corinthians 6:14-17, MSG*

I know that going against popular thinking can be difficult. But at some point, we've got to get away from the infection.

WE LET THE DEVIL ACCUSE US

A battle is raging all around you. You may not even be aware of it—but the battle is in your mind.

The devil's number one target is your thoughts. He knows that if he can get you to believe his lies, he'll be able to control and manipulate your life. Jesus said in John 8:44, "When he lies, he speaks his native language, for he is a liar and the father of lies." And when you believe the lie, you empower the liar. We have to overcome his accusations with better thoughts. This is why we must master our minds.

You are today where your thoughts have brought you, and you will go tomorrow where your thoughts take you.

It's time to start thinking about what you're thinking about. Proverbs 23:7 (NKJV) says, "For as he thinks in his heart, so is he." Let me give you five reasons why you need to master your mind.

1) Everything begins with a thought.

The things you're doing well and the things you're not doing well were first fueled by your thinking. In other words, if you try to change your behavior without changing the thoughts that fed that behavior, you'll never really change. Everything begins with a thought.

Adultery doesn't start without a thought.

Gossip doesn't start without a thought.

Hate doesn't start without a thought.

Greed doesn't start without a thought.

On the contrary, all life change begins with a thought. The growth and new life that God has for you begins with a thought. Look at Romans 12:2 again: "Do not conform to the pattern of this world, but be transformed by the renewing of your mind." God wants to give you a new way to think.

2) What we think determines how we feel.

Do you realize that your mind can affect how your body feels? You will speak, act, and react as the person you think you are. What we think determines how we feel.

You may be blaming it on your spouse, your teachers, your neighbors, or the economy. But trust me, they are not responsible for why you feel the way you do. Your response to those things—your thought life—is determining how you feel.

3) Our thoughts determine our destiny.

Sow a thought, reap an action. Sow an action, reap a habit. Sow a habit, reap a lifestyle. Sow a lifestyle, reap your destiny.

If you don't like where you're going, change your thought. Let me say it this way. You are today where your thoughts have brought you, and you will go tomorrow where your thoughts take you. If you see yourself as a loser, you end up, to a large degree, acting like a loser. If you see yourself as a victim, you tend to let people victimize you.

But on the other hand, if you see yourself as a child of God, filled with the Holy Spirit, set free, an overcomer, fully healed, protected by angels, first and not last, above and not beneath—you will walk in the direction your thoughts are pointed.

This isn't just the power of positive thinking. This is the Word of God!

> *Those who are dominated by the sinful nature* **think** *about sinful things, but those who are controlled by the Holy Spirit* **think** *about things that please the Spirit. So letting your sinful nature* **control your mind** *leads to death. But letting the Spirit* **control your mind** *leads to life and peace. —Romans 8:5-6, NLT* (**author emphasis**)

So, who has control of your mind?

The reality is, there is a battle for your mind happening right now.

THE BATTLEFIELD OF THE MIND

Your thoughts are a battlefield, and if you are going to remain free, you must learn to master your mind. This is accomplished through demolishing *strongholds* and taking your thoughts captive.

For though we walk in the flesh, we are not waging war according to the flesh. For the weapons of our warfare are not of the flesh but have divine power to destroy strongholds. We destroy arguments and every lofty opinion raised against the knowledge of God, and take every thought captive to obey Christ. —2 Corinthians 10:3-5, ESV

Many thoughts are dispatched by Satan to terrorize our faith. We need to master our minds and hold these thoughts captive in order to interrogate and destroy them. We need to screen every thought that comes into our minds to find where it came from. Did it come from the Kingdom of Heaven, or was it dispatched from the pit of Hell?

The weapon of the enemy is a lie. With negative thoughts, suspicions, doubts, fears, and worries, he bombards our minds. But since his weapon is a lie, the only thing that will counteract it is the truth. The truth has the power to bring freedom. Jesus declared, "Then you will know the truth, and the truth will set you free" (John 8:32).

Since the mind is a battlefield, let's look at four areas of our thought life that we need to guard.

1) Guard your mind against lies.

We are told we have divine power to demolish strongholds (2 Corinthians 10:3). The word "*strongholds*" in Greek is *ochurama*. It literally means any lie of the devil that keeps you trapped—any lie that is against God's word—that becomes a reality in your life just by believing it. Lies about ourselves, lies about others, and even lies about God. The devil will try to get you to believe things that are not true. He will try to get you to imagine things that you begin to believe.

We must be disciplined in the word of God so that we can recognize the lie when the enemy tells it. The problem is that we don't have the reference point of truth to stand in contrast to the lie. And the enemy is really skilled at making the lie sound really good. Remember, the apostle Paul tells us that "Satan himself masquerades as an Angel of light" (2 Corinthians 11:14). The lie the devil tells isn't always evil. He's going to tell you a lie that makes you feel good.

2) Guard your mind against fear.

Fear is a powerful force that can grip our hearts and paralyze our actions. It seeks to control and limit us, hindering our walk of freedom and our relationship with God. As believers, we are called to guard our minds against fear and to fully trust in God's promises and faithfulness.

The Apostle Paul reminds us in 2 Timothy 1:7 (NKJV), "For God has not given us a spirit of fear, but of power and of love and of a sound mind." This scripture reassures us that fear does not come from God but rather from the enemy who desires to steal our peace and confidence. It is essential for us to continually renew our minds with the truth of God's Word and to combat fear with faith.

One powerful Scripture that guides us in guarding our minds against fear is Philippians 4:6-7. The Apostle Paul writes, "Do not be anxious about anything, but in every situation, by prayer and petition, with thanksgiving, present your requests to God. And the peace of God, which transcends all understanding, will guard your hearts and your minds in Christ Jesus." Paul encourages us to bring our worries and fears before God in prayer and thanksgiving, trusting that He will provide us with His peace that surpasses all human understanding.

By surrendering our fears to God and seeking His presence, we allow His peace to guard our hearts and minds, shielding us from the torment of fear.

3) Guard your mind against temptation.

Guarding what fills our minds is a daily battle. With access to the internet, television, movies, music, and books everywhere we go, we need to fill our minds with truth, not poison. Nutritionists will tell you that there are three kinds of food: brain food, junk food, and toxic food.

There is junk food. It doesn't even have to be bad food; it could just be empty calories we fill up on. It tastes good but just adds weight. There are things that take up space in our minds. They don't have to be bad—they may just be empty calories taking up weight and space.

Then there is toxic food. We don't realize it is toxic as we consume it. I mean, it looks good. But immediately after eating it, you can feel it going directly to your love handles. This food clogs the arteries. Toxic food will kill you. Toxic thoughts will destroy you.

We need to fill our minds with the right things.

4) Guard your mind against negativity.

Negativity has a way of creeping into our minds, poisoning our thoughts, and affecting our outlook on life. However, as believers, we have the power to guard our minds against negativity and fill our thoughts with that which is good, pure, and praiseworthy. The Apostle Paul gives us clear instructions in Philippians 4:8, "Finally, brothers and sisters, whatever is true, whatever is noble, whatever is right, whatever is pure, whatever is lovely, whatever is admirable—if anything is excellent or praiseworthy—think about such things." This

Scripture reminds us to intentionally focus our minds on positive and uplifting thoughts. By deliberately shifting our attention towards the goodness of God, the blessings in our lives, and the virtues of others, we create a mental atmosphere that fosters joy, gratitude, and positivity.

As we commit ourselves to guard our minds against negativity, let us cling to these scriptures and allow them to shape our thought patterns. By intentionally filling our minds with positive and God-honoring thoughts, we can experience a renewed perspective, an increased sensitivity to His presence, and a deeper sense of peace and joy in our lives. Let us choose to guard our minds, take hold of every thought, and fix our focus on the things that bring honor and glory to God.

HOW TO HAVE TRANSFORMED THINKING

Changed thinking and mastering our minds will not happen automatically. It's going to take time, effort, and intentionality, but it will forever change your life and set you up for a life of freedom. How do you master your mind and transform your thinking? Let me give you five ways.

1) Make a plan for controlling your thoughts.

Some of us are being fed bad thinking. Most of it is coming through the internet and the things we are exposing ourselves to. The information and content we are consuming to entertain and inform us is poisoning our thoughts.

You have to find a plan to control your thoughts, and the best way to do this is to read the Bible. It's amazing to me how when you read the Bible, it changes how you think. Don't read the Bible out of discipline;

read it to consume it. Just watch how it will take every negative, destructive, and demonic thought that puts you down and replace it with how God sees you.

The Word of God is powerful! In fact, the Bible is not like any other book. This book breathes; it has a heartbeat; it has power. Hebrews 4:12 (author emphasis) says, "For the word of God is living and active. Sharper than any double-edged sword, it penetrates even to dividing *soul* and *spirit*, joints and marrow; it judges the *thoughts* and *attitudes* of the heart."

Don't read the Bible, let the Bible read you.

The soul is the intellectual, mental, and emotional part of you. The spirit is the part of you that can connect and commune with God. The reason why our thinking needs to be transformed is because we are living from our natural mind, feeling, intellect, and reason instead of walking in the Spirit. We are meshing the soul and the spirit, leaving us unable to distinguish our feelings from the wisdom of Heaven.

The Word of God is the sharp instrument of God that allows us to separate that which is divine inside of us and that which is carnal. So, when you're living in this world and there are problems, chores, crying kids, and demanding bosses, the Word of God has divided those emotions from my spirit so that divine life can still flow from me, no matter what's happening around me.

And if you'll let the Word of God work, it will divide the soul and spirit and allow you to judge rightly the thoughts and attitudes of your heart. I like to say it this way: Don't read the Bible, let the Bible read you. It will change you.

2) Find a place to think your thoughts.

At some point in your day, the volume of the world has to be turned down. Even if it's just for five minutes, put your focus on God. You have to have a place to let God speak to you as you are speaking to God. If you want to master your mind, have a daily conversation with God.

Now listen, God does not want your formality. He doesn't need it to rhyme, and He doesn't need it in the King James Version. Just talk to Him in your normal voice. Talk to him like He's in the room and He's actually interested in what you have to say. Slow your life down long enough to have a daily conversation with God.

If time is an issue, just start with a sentence. Of course, I want you to pray without ceasing, but some of us just need to start somewhere. Just acknowledge Him. He'd rather hear that than nothing at all. Isaiah 26:3 (NLT) says, "You will keep in perfect peace all who trust in you, all whose thoughts are fixed on you! Let me say it another way. Those who cast all of their problems, cares, and issues onto Him, who trust Him, who make that time for prayer—God will keep in perfect peace.

Colossians 3:2 (NLT) says, "Think about the things of heaven, not the things of earth." If you don't have a moment in your day to think about heaven instead of earth, you're probably going to register low on the peace meter.

3) Find the right people to stretch your thoughts.

In the pursuit of mastering our minds, finding the right people to surround ourselves with is crucial. Proverbs 13:20 tells us, "Walk with the wise and become wise, for a companion of fools suffers harm." It is essential to seek out individuals who share in our desires for growth, freedom, and alignment with God's truth. Surrounding ourselves with wise and like-minded individuals not only influences our thought patterns but also provides a network of support, encouragement, and accountability on our journey towards mastering our minds.

But finding the right people goes beyond seeking those who merely share our aspirations. It also involves discerning individuals who are authentic, supportive, and aligned with biblical values. First Corinthians 15:33 warns us, "Do not be misled: 'Bad company corrupts good character.'" We must be discerning in who we choose to be our companions. We need to surround ourselves with people whose influence on our minds and spirits is positive and uplifting. Connections with individuals who genuinely care about our well-being can help us navigate the challenges and obstacles that come with mastering our minds.

Additionally, finding the right people involves seeking mentors and spiritual guides who can provide wisdom, guidance, and accountability. Proverbs 27:17 reminds us, "As iron sharpens iron, so one person sharpens another." The presence of mentors and spiritual guides in our lives can significantly impact our journey toward mastering our minds. They can provide valuable insights, challenge our thinking, and hold us accountable to living in alignment with God's truth.

The company we keep reflects the state of our minds and hearts.

Hebrews 10:24-25 encourages us to consider how we can spur one another toward love and good deeds by not giving up on gathering together, as some are in the habit of doing. The verse emphasizes the importance of gathering with like-minded believers and investing in relationships that strengthen our faith and encourage positive thinking. By coming together in fellowship and community, we create an environment where we can uplift one another, share our struggles and victories, and inspire each other to stay committed to our journey of freedom. Through this unity, we find support, accountability, and the opportunity to learn from the wisdom and experiences of others.

Proverbs 27:19 states, "As water reflects the face, so one's life reflects the heart." The company we keep reflects the state of our minds and hearts. By choosing to surround ourselves with wise, positive, and authentic individuals, we align ourselves with God's truth, empower our journey of transformation, and create a supportive and inspiring community that uplifts our mental and spiritual well-being. Get around the right people.

4) Find a purpose to land your thoughts.

The healthiest thoughts you can have are thoughts about why you're on this planet.—thoughts about your eternal purpose for God's kingdom. When you can think, "I know this is bad, I know this is a challenge, but I know why I'm here! I know why I'm fighting! I've got a job to do!", you will order your thoughts according to God's plan and purpose for your life, no matter what you're facing.

The most miserable people I know are not circumstantially miserable. The most miserable people are the ones who don't know why in the world they're on this planet. They don't know their purpose.

Let's go back to Romans 12:2 and pull in verse 3: "Do not conform to the pattern of this world, but be transformed by the renewing of your mind. **THEN** you will be able to test and approve what God's will is—his good, pleasing and perfect will" (author emphasis).

When you allow God to change your thinking and you begin to master your mind, THEN you will know God's will for your life! The reason why I have passion and determination is because I know exactly why I'm on this planet. I'm not wandering aimlessly, and I'm not easily thwarted from my target. I have a purpose for living, and I want that so badly for you. So now we have this purpose stirring inside of us, and you're going to have to . . .

5) Find the power to fuel your thoughts.

As followers of Jesus, we have access to an incredible source of power—the Holy Spirit. The Holy Spirit is the third person of the Trinity, and He dwells within us, guiding, empowering, and transforming our thoughts and actions. Romans 8:6 reminds us that "The mind governed by the flesh is death, but the mind governed by the Spirit is life and peace." When we allow the Holy Spirit to take control of our minds, our thoughts align with God's truth, leading to a life filled with peace, joy, and purpose.

The Holy Spirit plays a vital role in transforming our thought patterns. He enables us to discern between truth and lies and empowers us to reject negative and destructive thinking. Galatians 5:22-23 tells us that the fruit of the Spirit includes love, joy, peace, patience, kindness, goodness, faithfulness, gentleness, and self-control. By inviting the Holy Spirit to work in our minds, we begin to cultivate these qualities in our thoughts, which ultimately shape our words and actions.

When we rely on the power of the Holy Spirit, we gain access to divine wisdom and revelation. First Corinthians 2:12 tells us, "What we have received is not the spirit of the world, but the Spirit who is from God, so that we may understand what God has freely given us." The Holy Spirit illuminates our minds, enabling us to grasp and apply God's truths, leading to renewed thinking and a transformed mindset. As we deepen our relationship with the Holy Spirit through prayer, meditation on God's Word, and surrendering our thoughts to Him, we open ourselves up to God's incredible power.

The Holy Spirit provides comfort, peace, and strength amid challenging and negative circumstances. When we face difficult thoughts or experiences, the Holy Spirit is our advocate and helper, empowering us to overcome negativity and renew our minds. Romans 15:13 proclaims, "May the God of hope fill you with all joy and peace as you trust in him, so that you may overflow with hope by the power of the Holy Spirit." With the Holy Spirit's guidance, we can choose to focus on hope, joy, and positive thoughts, even in the midst of adversity, knowing that God's power is at work within us.

Do you have the power of the Holy Spirit fueling your thoughts and life? You can by doing three things.

Remove the barriers: Repent and come to God completely. Surrender your whole life.

Request the gift of the Holy Spirit: Ask God to fill you with His Holy Spirit.

Receive Him by faith: Trust that Jesus will do what He said He would do, and send the Holy Spirit to fill and empower you (Luke 11:13).

The power of the Holy Spirit will help you master your mind, but His power and help are necessary to accomplish step seven in our freedom journey—opposing a culture of idolatry.

STEP 7

OPPOSING A CULTURE OF IDOLATRY

More than 1,000 verses speak of this topic. More than fifty of the laws in the first five books of the Bible directly address it. In Judaism, it was one of only four sins to which the death penalty was attached. Yet we skip over it as an antiquated or irrelevant issue. But nothing could be further from the truth. It's the war that is being waged for our worship. The Bible calls it idolatry. These are the gods at war within each of us. They battle for the place of glory in our lives. And there's a lot at stake because whichever god is victorious is the god who wins control and power over us.

Underneath every sin is a false god that is sitting on the throne of your heart—and until that god is dethroned, you won't have victory.

Ultimately, the god you choose determines your destiny.

A CULTURE OF IDOLS

On the surface, it doesn't seem like we really struggle with idols. But this is, in fact, *the* struggle. You might say, "I struggle with being anxious and worried." But why is that?

An idol is anything that takes the focus off God and puts it on something else.

Maybe it's because you've made comfort and security your god. If you keep losing your battle with lust, maybe it's because sex is your god. If you struggle with legalism, maybe religious rules are your false god. If you're discontent, maybe you've made money your god. If you lack self-control, maybe pleasure has become your god. Underneath every sin is a false god that is sitting on the throne of your heart—and until that god is dethroned, you won't have victory.

See, an idol is anything that takes the focus off God and puts it on something else. When anything is first in my life that is not God, it's an idol, even if it's good. Romans 1:25 (GNT) says, "They exchange the truth about God for a lie; they worship and serve what God has created instead of the Creator himself!"

Let me show you that well-known verse in the Ten Commandments about idolatry:

I am the Lord your God, who rescued you from the land of Egypt, the place of your slavery. You must not have any other god but me. You must not make for yourself an idol of any kind or an image of anything in the heavens or on the earth or in the sea. You must not

bow down to them or worship them, for I, the Lord your God, am
a jealous God who will not tolerate your affection for any other
gods! —*Exodus 20:2-5, NLT*

What does it mean to idolize? In this sense, it means to value something more than God. Some people park their idols in their garages. Some people put their idols in their safe deposit boxes. But even today, we have to deal with idols. It's interesting; archaeologists tell us in every culture throughout history there have been idols. Statues, little gods, goddesses—things like that. For some reason, man desires to turn objects or people or things into objects of worship.

In Bible times there were three primary idols. There was Baal who was the god of sex. There was Mammon who was the god of money. And there was Molech who was the god of violence. We don't have those metal idols today—we just pay billions of dollars to go to movies to watch sex, violence, and money. It's the same thing.

Someone may say, "well I don't bow down and worship any idols." Okay, if that's true, then ask yourself this question.

WHERE IS YOUR SANCTUARY?

Where do you go when you're hurting? Let's say it's been a terrible day at the office. You come home and go—where? To the refrigerator for comfort food like ice cream? To the phone to vent with your most trusted friend? Do you seek escape in novels or movies or video games or pornography? Where do you look for emotional rescue?

The Bible tells us that God is our refuge and strength, our help in times of trouble, so much so that we will not fear though the mountains fall into the heart of the sea (Psalm 46:1-2). That strikes me as a good place to run. But it's so easy to forget, so easy for us to run in other directions. Where we go says a lot about who we are. The "high ground" we seek reveals the geography of our values.

The "high ground" we seek reveals the geography of our values.

Deuteronomy 4:15-16 (GNT) says, "For your own good, then, make certain that you do not sin by making for yourselves an idol in any form at all." This suggests that they do come in many forms. God says, for your own good, don't idolize anything or anyone. Let me give you three reasons why.

Idols Will Disappoint You.

They always promise more than they can deliver. The TV says, "wear our label and you'll be popular," "buy our product and you'll be successful," "drink our beer—it won't get any better than that," "buy our toothpaste and you'll have sex appeal." They always promise more than they can deliver. Jeremiah 10:14 (GNT) says, "Those who make idols are disillusioned, because the gods they make are false and lifeless."

Have you ever ordered something through a mail order catalog and when you got it you were disappointed with what you got? Anytime you put any person, anything, or any product in the place of God, you will be disappointed. Anytime you expect someone to solve all your problems or guarantee happiness, you're going to be disappointed. Idols will always disappoint you.

Idols Will Dominate You.

If you don't watch out for them, they end up controlling your life. First Corinthians 12 says, "When you were pagans, somehow or other you were influenced and led astray to mute idols." It says there are two inevitable effects when you love something more than God:

1) Whatever you love more than God will begin to control you. The word we use a lot today for idols is the word "addiction". You can be addicted to your work, to sex, to sports, to numerous things besides alcohol or drugs. But eventually, it runs your life when you love something more than you love God. People say, "I can give it up at any time." Then why don't you do it now? If you don't, it will dominate and distract your life.

2) It says you will be led astray. You lose your perspective when something takes place in your life that ought to be where God is. How many people, by the lure of a promotion, were led to neglect their family at a crucial time in their kids' lives? How many people compromised their integrity for the promise of fame? How many people have thrown their convictions out the door because of a profit incentive? God says if you don't watch out, an idol, anything that you love more than God, will distract you and you will lose your values.

You may have never realized this, but if you allow someone to control your life by waiting on their approval or disapproval and choosing what's right for you, that's not just co-dependency—that's called idolatry. It's making that person a god. The number one way to break a co-dependency is to 1) put God first in your life and 2) give your ultimate devotion to Him and no one else.

Here's the third reason.

Idols Will Deform You.

Idols will change you. They'll warp you. You'll lose the uniqueness that God gave you because *you become like what you value the most*. Psalm 115:8 says, "Those who make them [idols] will be like them, and so will all who trust in them." We shape an idol, and it ends up shaping us. You will become like whatever is first place in your life, so you better reserve that spot for God or you're going to get deformed. You will be misshapen, unable to be what God meant for you to be in the first place.

You'll never get the best of God until He has all of you.

One time a rich young ruler came to Jesus. He said, "What must I do to follow Christ? What must I do to have eternal life?" Jesus responded, "Go, sell everything you've got and give it to the poor, and come follow me." It's interesting that not one other time in the Bible did Jesus say that to anybody. He only said it to him. Why? Because Jesus knew what the idol of his life was—his bank account. He went straight to the heart of the issue and said, "You've got another god in your life, and if you really want to follow Me, give up what you've got, and come, follow Me." The Scripture says that this guy counted the cost, decided it wasn't worth it, and walked away (see Matthew 19:21-22).

What do you need to give up? What is it that you're holding on to that's keeping you from being all God wants you to be? There may be a relationship you need to let go of that you won't, even though you know it's not right. You may know you are in a career that is not right for you but you're still holding on to it. You may be holding onto a habit that you know is hurting you. Those are idols. If God tells you to give up something and you can't let go of it, then you don't own it—it owns you.

Idols will distract you, dominate you, disappoint you, and eventually destroy you if you don't stay alert. So, God says, "For your own good, don't let anything get first place in your life—a career, girlfriend, dream—not anything. Keep Me in first place."

I see a lot of people who try to follow God or investigate faith little by little. They put a toe in the water. And that's okay. I believe church should be a place where you can feel free to investigate your unique journey with God.

They know how to follow the rules, but they don't really know how to follow Jesus.

But this thing called Christianity doesn't really work unless you're ALL IN. You'll never get the best of God until He has all of you. And that's the truth. Joshua challenged the people, "Consecrate yourselves, for tomorrow the Lord will do amazing things among you" (Joshua 3:5). To "consecrate" simply means to fully devote. When you fully devote, you will see God move powerfully in your life.

In Matthew 4:19, Jesus issued the invitation, "Come, follow me." Many people misinterpret what Jesus meant by this. They know how to follow the rules, but they don't really know how to follow Jesus. As a result, many haven't accepted this invitation because they feel like they don't measure up.

But Jesus is not calling us to total perfection. The disciples surely weren't perfect. Actually, they were perfectly flawed. He isn't calling us to total perfection, He's simply calling us to total devotion. And that's what it means to follow Jesus. Not rules, not dos and don'ts. It's about your heart. He wants *you*. The apostle Paul gave a good description of what it looks like to go all in in his letter to the Romans.

> *So here's what I want you to do, God helping you: Take your everyday, ordinary life— your sleeping, eating, going-to-work, and walking-around life—and place it before God as an offering. Embracing what God does for you is the best thing that you can do for him. Don't become so well adjusted to your culture that you fit into it without even thinking. Instead, fix your attention on God. You'll be changed from the inside out. Readily recognize what he wants from you, and quickly respond to it. Unlike the culture around you, always dragging you down to its level of immaturity, God brings the best out of you, develops well-formed maturity in you. —Romans 12:1-2, MSG*

God wants all of you—the good, the bad, the ugly. What He wants is your everyday, ordinary life. One translation says, "Don't conform to the pattern of this world. . . ." (Romans 12:2). But if you want to be a kingdom citizen, someone who's fully devoted to God, you need to know there is a different culture that we need to operate in. It is counterculture. And we develop it by fixing our attention on God. When you do that, Paul says you'll be changed from the inside out. You'll be able to readily recognize what God wants you to do.

Many of us feel the tension between the two cultures at war with each other. We hear the invitation, "Come, follow me," but we also feel the pull of the world. And like Paul said, the culture around you wants to drag you down to its level of immaturity. And most of us feel that; we feel culture pulling us down—away from the will of God. When you are far from His will, you are close to becoming a slave to a culture that does not want freedom for you.

He isn't calling us to total perfection, He's simply calling us to total devotion.

But God wants to bring you to full maturity. The way to get there is by going all in with God, to live a fully devoted life. How do we live fully devoted to God in a culture and society that does not want God involved in anything? We have to figure out how to live for God in an ungodly world. Let's look to the book of Daniel for help.

THE CULTURE AROUND YOU

Daniel and his friends had the challenge of living for God in an ungodly culture that was full of idol worship, just as ours is. This true story takes place in about 600 BC. King Nebuchadnezzar was the greatest king of Babylon, which was located in modern-day Iraq and spread to contain most of the Middle East. Jerusalem was located 870 miles due west of the city of Babylon. As you know, Israel went through periods when they were fully devoted to God, and God had favor on them. But time and again, they would join with the cultures around them and turn their backs on God, worshipping the false idols of the neighboring nations. Then God would warn them through the prophets, and if they didn't repent, He'd use some powerful nation to conquer Israel and show them just how powerless their false idols were and how great His favor had been. Babylon was one of those conquering nations.

King Nebuchadnezzar came and besieged Jerusalem and tore it apart and, like a fisherman throwing out a long net, gathered most of the nobles residing in Jerusalem where the king's palace was, as well as most of the rest of the population of Judah, carrying them off into captivity. The Bible calls this "exile" because it wasn't the might of Babylon that came and stole them away; it was God who used the might of Babylon to exile His unfaithful people from their home until they repented. And just like many different fish get caught up in a fishing net, those who still worshipped the Lord were caught up together with those who worshipped idols. Daniel and his three friends were among those who worshipped the Lord.

This story of Daniel takes place in the land of their exile. The four young men are in the enemy's capital city. They know God, they love God, and they want to live for God, but they've been dropped into a culture that does not know God, that worships gods made by their own hands, that engages in vile acts, that expects them to do what they do. The men of Judah are feeling the tension. So what do they do?

In the third year of the reign of Jehoiakim king of Judah, Nebu-chadnezzar king of Babylon came to Jerusalem and besieged it. And the Lord delivered Jehoiakim, king of Judah into his hand, along with some of the articles from the temple of God. These he carried off to the temple of his god in Babylonia and put it in the treasure house of his god.

Then the king ordered Ashpenaz, chief of his court officials, to bring into the king's service some of the Israelites from the royal family and the nobility—young men without any physical defect, handsome, showing aptitude for every kind of learning, well informed, quick to understand, and qualified to serve in the king's palace.

He was to teach them the language and literature of the Babylonians. The king assigned them a daily amount of food and wine from the king's table. They were to be trained for three years, and after that they were to enter the king's service.

Among those who were chosen were some from Judah: Daniel, Hananiah, Mishael, and Azariah. The chief official gave them new names: to Daniel, the name Balteshazzar; to Hananiah, Shadrach; to Mishael, Meshach; and to Azariah, Abednego. —Daniel 1:1-6

Ashpenaz, the chief of Nebuchadnezzar's court officials, was told to pick out the cream of the crop, the best and brightest of the noble prisoners from Israel and teach them the ways of Babylon. He was also given a diet plan for the prisoners to follow. Now that's important because the Jews had certain dietary restrictions and laws, and there were things on the king's table that they would allocate for them to eat and drink that they were not supposed to eat and drink. So here are these four young men who are in much worse shape than we're in. Our culture may punish those who don't comply, but the Babylonians would hardly blink at killing a prisoner who wouldn't comply, in truly horrific ways. These guys had no control over their lives, their surroundings, or their persons. Yet, they figured out how to live for God in an ungodly culture.

What are you going to do when culture contradicts your convictions? Or let me say it this way: What are you going to do when culture changes? Will you change with it?

Culture is in continuous flux, but God never changes.

Don't try to modify God to fit your culture. We need to be modified to fit God's will.

There are three ways that culture tries to win our hearts to other gods if we allow it to.

CULTURE WILL TRY TO RENAME YOU

Our enemy isn't creative or innovative. But he's persistent. He's still using the same tactics now that he used almost 3,000 years ago in Daniel's time. Let me show you what I mean. In Daniel 1:7, picking up the story where we left off, the chief official, Ashpenaz, gave them Babylonian names: Belteshazzar, Shadrach, Meshach, and Abednago.

Don't try to modify God to fit your culture. We need to be modified to fit God's will.

The first goal of culture is to *rename* you. Culture wants to change your identity from who God made you to be to who the world wants you to be. And it's a direct attack on your God-given destiny. You may still be living the labels that other people have put on you—your diagnosis, hurtful words, etc. And you're carrying this label around and either trying to live up to it or live out of it. But it's not who God says you are. The comparison between the four Hebrew names to the four Babylonian names they were given is frightening.

Daniel means "God is my judge." Conversely, Belteshazzar means "Baal protects my life." Baal was the name of the Babylonian god. Culture renames us so that we will place our hope, security, and fulfillment in things other than God. They then become an idol in our lives. Isn't that the definition of control? The pursuit of idols masquerades as freedom—you get to do what you want on your own terms. But really, you are willingly handing over legal authority of your life to a world that wants nothing more than to uproot you from the freedom that is found only in God. You are choosing to be controlled and renamed as Jane Doe #8923 made in the image of the world. You have been marked as ordinary, just another pawn in the enemy's game. But God says you are unique and set apart.

Hananiah means "Yahweh has been gracious." But Shadrach means, "I am fearful of God." The world changes "God has good for you" to "God is bad; you don't want to serve Him." We know which one is the truth.

Now Michael means "Who is what God is?" which basically means, "There is no one like my God!" Mishach means, "I am despised, contemptible, and humiliated."

We see this happening in our culture today; the focus is shifting from confidence to insecurity. Worldly culture discourages discourse about the Christian faith and twists the truth of the Word of God. (Separation from church and state does not mean that church and state should not touch or intersect. It means the church needs protection from the infringement of the government.) The world wants to make cowards who are afraid to share and live out their faith. It's meant to separate us from one another because the enemy knows that there's encouragement in numbers.

Finally, Azariah means, "Yahweh has helped." And that term, Yahweh, was a very personal name for God. It was so precious that the writers of the scriptures used a special utensil. It wasn't used much because it was so personal. Conversely, Abednego meant "servant of Nebo." Nebo was one of their false gods. Culture tries to shift our focus from sonship to slavery so that we follow the rules of a religious system.

When culture contradicts your convictions, you need to know who you actually are in Christ.

CULTURE WILL TRY TO TAME YOU

Culture wants to lure you into faulty narratives: "It's not going to hurt anyone." "I certainly don't want to be in conflict with everybody." "We have to live in this world." We end up compromising our convictions. Culture is continually trying to tame you—or you might say, house train you.

When culture contradicts your convictions, you need to hold to them even tighter. You need to know the Word of God, know the Holy Spirit, and follow God.

Daniel 1:9 says, "Now God had caused the official to show favor and compassion to Daniel." Ashpenaz doesn't slap him to the ground and tell him he's going to eat the food and like it. The official returns respect for respect and admits, "I am afraid of my lord the king, who has assigned your food and drink. Why should he see you looking worse than the other young men your age? The king would then have my head because of you" (v. 10). It was his belief that the king's food was the best in the land. If you ate it, you'd actually be stronger, healthier, and smarter. They weren't trying to poison the prisoners; they were trying to nurture them to the best of their ability. And they didn't have any respect, yet, for the Israelite God. Ashpenaz had plenty of respect for the king, though, and wouldn't risk his head.

> *Daniel then said to the guard whom the chief official had appointed over Daniel, Hananiah, Mishael, and Azariah, 'Please test your servants for ten days. Give us nothing but vegetables to eat and water to drink. Then compare our appearance with that of the young men who eat the royal food, and treat your servants in accordance with what you see.' So he agreed to this and tested them for ten days. —verses 11–14*

Here's what I want you to know: If you're going to be fully devoted and live all in for God in this ungodly culture in which we live, you will be tested. You will have pressure points along your journey. You'll come to defining moments in your walk of faith. Holy Spirit is not the only spirit that will tug you.

CULTURE WILL TRY TO CLAIM YOU

Culture wants to claim you as its own. There is a battle for your soul happening right now. You have been given the deciding vote. Who are you going to allow to claim you?

"So he [the guard] agreed to this and tested them for ten days. At the end of the ten days, they looked healthier and better nourished than any of the young men who ate the royal food. So the guard took away their choice food and the wine they were to drink and gave them vegetables instead" (v. 14-16). Then the scripture shows how God honors their devotion to Him by bringing the best out of them: "To these four young men God gave knowledge and understanding of all kinds of literature and learning. And Daniel could understand visions and dreams of all kinds" (v. 17).

Three years later, the chief official presented them to Nebuchadnezzar. The king talked with them and found none equal to them. Verse 20 picks up the tale: "In every matter of wisdom and understanding about which the king questioned them, he found them ten times better than all the magicians and enchanters in his whole kingdom." Living your life as a claimed child of God will always be ten times better.

CULTURE TESTS US

In Daniel's time, noncompliance to following an ungodly culture was a sure path to death. This was the first test for Daniel and the three boys. They had been made administrators over the province of Babylon while

Daniel was busy elsewhere. It started when King Nebuchadnezzar had his artisans create an enormous gold statue. It was about 90 in. high and 9 in. wide. Then he called all of the officials, from the satraps who were his right-hand men to the least of the provincial officials to come to the dedication of his new god.

When they were assembled, he had his royal decree loudly proclaimed that as soon as they heard the signal from the musicians, they were all to fall down and worship this idol. "Whoever does not fall down and worship will immediately be thrown into a blazing furnace" (Daniel 3:6). These guys were faced with life and death, but they firmly declared, "We will not bow down." When the musicians signaled, everyone bowed down except for Shadrach, Meschah, and Abednego.

Your faith is worthless if it only stands up when you get your way.

The King gave them a second chance to bow down and worship. He couldn't believe that these prisoners whom he'd exalted to high positions in his government wouldn't obey him. He said, "Let's try this again, and then what god will be able to rescue you from my hand?" And in Daniel 3:16-18, he got his answer.

Shadrach, Meshach, and Abednego replied to him, 'King Nebuchadnezzar, we do not need to defend ourselves before you in this matter. If we are thrown into the blazing furnace, the God we serve is able to deliver us from it, and he will deliver us from Your Majesty's hand. But even if he does not, we want you to know, Your

Majesty, that we will not serve your gods or worship the image of
gold you have set up.

Your faith is worthless if it only stands up when you get your way.

You need a "but-even-if" kind of faith; you need a faith that shows up when the door closes. You need a faith that shows up when you're facing the fire—when you're in the dark.

So how do we pass the test of culture?

NEW FACES AND NEW PLACES

Number one, you've got to get around some new faces and new places. In fact, this was a tactic that the Babylonians used when they besieged Israel and Judah; they took the best and brightest away from their homes and families and immersed them in Babylonian culture among Babylonian people. This tactic is called acculturation. They knew that if they took the Jews out of their familiar surroundings and away from their own kind who had the same beliefs, traditions, and habits, and dropped them into completely new places full of new faces and new customs, little by little they would lose their values, their beliefs, their customs, their traditions.

There's no way around it—you've got to get around some new faces and new places who are living lives marked by true freedom. Jesus invited us to come and follow Him to a whole new kingdom. For the Hebrew people, Jesus was a new face teaching about a new place—the kingdom of God.

DON'T RUN FROM THE FIRE

Daniel's story illustrates it best—don't run from the fire. That doesn't mean play with fire. Too many Christians are playing with fire. They try to see how close they can get to the flames without being burned. God's fire is not there to burn or destroy you. It's there to perfect you.

It's there to release you from the grip of worldly ownership, not submerge or drown you in a life of fear and pain.

When the world sees you lean into your troubles but they do not consume you, they will be attracted to that flame.

In Daniel 3:24-25, Nebuchadnezzar was furious with Shadrack, Mesheck, and Abednego because they would not bow down and worship the designated statue, and his attitude towards them changed. He ordered the furnace to be heated seven times hotter than usual and commanded some of his strongest soldiers to tie up three Hebrew offenders and throw them into the blazing furnace. And they did. Then, King Nebuchadnezzar leaped to his feet in amazement and asked his advisors, "weren't there three men that were tied up that we threw into the fire?" And they said, "certainly, you're majesty."

The king then said, "Look, I see four men walking around in the fire, unbound and unharmed, and the fourth looks like the son of the gods." You see, God does his greatest work *in* the fire. Many Christians want the faith of Shadrach, Meshach, and Abednego, but they don't want to step into the fiery furnace. Yet, the fire is where great faith is formed.

So, stop running from the flames—lean into them.

Think about the upper room. Jesus told His followers that they shouldn't try to change this world without Holy Spirit fire. And after a while, they prayed and the Holy Spirit rested on them, and they were filled with the Holy Spirit. Then, they went out and turned the world upside down for God's glory.

Idols are defeated not by being removed, but by being replaced.

The Bible says that the bush Moses saw was burning *but not consumed.* Moses's response was to move *toward* the fire. You see, when the world sees you lean *into* your troubles but they do not consume you, they will be attracted to that flame. It's one of the most powerful forms of Christian witness. It gives you a divine opportunity to tell people all about the fourth man in the fire—Jesus, the Son of God.

URGENCY AND PURPOSE

Here's number three—we need to live with a sense of *purpose* and *urgency.* Our days are literally numbered. We are not promised today. We are not promised tomorrow. If we want to live an all-in-for-God kind of life, then we need to cultivate and maintain a sense of purpose and urgency. The prisoner who longs for freedom serves his time with a sense of urgency—he takes it seriously. We've all heard the rags to riches stories—the convict, a menace to society—who submerged a completely different man. That man invited the hope of his freedom into that jail cell, day in and day out, and pursued it with a sense of urgency.

God loves you and wants to do something in you and through you. You have the best gift that you can give yourself: to know your purpose and live it out. If you do that, you will resolve 99 percent of your problems. It doesn't mean that the fire is not going to be there. It doesn't mean that the test won't come. It's just that you have found purpose in the pain. David put it this way:

Lord, make me to know my end,
And what is the measure of my days,
That I may know how frail I am.
Indeed, You have made my days as handbreadths,
And my age is as nothing before You;
Certainly every man at his best state is but vapor.
—Psalm 39:4-5, NKJV

An entire lifetime is just a moment to God. Human existence is but a breath to Him. So, we need to live with a sense of purpose and urgency.

WHY NOT GO ALL IN . . . NOW?

Idols are defeated not by being removed, but by being replaced. The question is, who will you serve? Joshua asks this question of the Hebrew people. He presented them with the same choice that we have today. In Joshua 24:14, he says, "Now fear the LORD and serve him with all faithfulness. Throw away the gods your forefathers worshiped beyond the Euphrates River and in Egypt, and serve the Lord." These were the gods from previous generations, gods from the past that never went away. See, the Hebrews were Egyptian slaves for longer than the United States has been a nation, and while they were there, they picked up some false idols. Old habits, including old worship patterns, die hard. Do you ever find yourself struggling with things from the past that you thought you had left behind a long time ago? Those things want your heart, but Joshua tells us to throw them away for good.

"But if serving the LORD seems undesirable to you, then choose for yourselves this day whom you will serve, whether the gods your ancestors served. . . ." (Joshua 24:15). This is the choice so many people default to. Who did your mom or dad worship? Did your dad worship sports, sex, money, status, or beer? Did your mom worship shopping, career, children, or entertainment? It is natural to choose the path of our parents by adopting their gods. Joshua states that one option is to choose "the gods of the Amorites, in whose land you are living." This is the god of the culture around you. The Israelites lived in a place where there was a lot of diversity, much like our society. There were many people groups and many different gods. And although we may not be confronted with Baal or Ashtoreth, two primary gods of their culture, we have cultural gods of our own, like pleasure, sex, success. Our idols are hiding in plain sight, and it is possible that we don't recognize them because they're so common.

Our idols are hiding in plain sight, and it is possible that we don't recognize them because they're so common.

Then Joshua gives a final option—the choice I'm encouraging you to make today. "But as for me and my household, we will serve the LORD." I want to encourage you to go all in *now*, not later. If God is good, and He has good for you, what are you waiting for? Why would you live on the fence?

Don't do Christianity halfway. Go all in with God. Make a commitment right now to give Him the next year fully devoted to Him. You have likely made other long-lasting commitments in your life for things of far less importance in comparison to God's will. You've given your time to dead-end careers. You've given time to hobbies. Why not give God the creator and sustainer of life one year of your full devotion and see if it's not at least ten times better?

The easiest way to go all in is just to say *yes*.

If there's a service, be there. If there's a prayer, pray it. If there's a worship night, experience it. Whatever it is, just do it. Give God everything and see what He can do in and through you. Like it says in Paul's second letter to the Corinthians: "Now is the time of God's favor, now is the day of salvation" (2 Corinthians 6:2).

It can be a little scary to go all in because it requires some level of sacrifice. What do you need to give up? It could be a relationship, a career, or a habit that may be pulling you away from the values that honor and glorify God. Remember, if God calls you to let go of something and you can't, then you don't own it. It owns you.

Identify the idols in your own life and then ask yourself this question: What kind of joy, fruitfulness, or inner fulfillment have they produced? If we are honest with ourselves, we would have to admit that they have taken so much more than they've given.

In Psalm 86:8, David says, "Among the gods there is none like you, Lord; no deeds can compare with yours." There's no contest between what God can offer and what the world offers. When Jesus extends the invitation to three different people to follow Him in Luke 9:23, on all three occasions, each one expressed the desire to, but none of them made the choice to. They all gave Jesus a "but first" and made excuses about why the timing wasn't right. You need to get off your "but first" and put God first in your life. Make Him your priority. Make Him your God. His throne only has one seat. Let me make this really practical for you. There are five areas in your life where you need to put God first and replace your idols.

1) Your Schedule

How you spend your time reveals what really has first place in your life. If I could see your calendar, would it reveal that God is first in your life? If I followed you around for one day, other than Sunday, would it reveal that God is the priority of your life?

In Psalm 5:3, David says, "In the morning, Lord, you hear my voice; in the morning I lay my requests before you and wait expectantly." If you really want to guard your heart from false idols, you need to put God first in your schedule.

Wake up in the morning and spend even just ten minutes with Him. It could be one sentence. "Good morning, God." Many of you are grossly overscheduled. You've said yes to so many other things that you can't say yes to God. Not only are you unable to say yes, but you see time with God as an inconvenience. When God presents you with an opportunity and you respond with "Oh, I just can't say yes to another thing." That's because you have said yes to the wrong things. But if you say yes to Him, God will create a margin in your life so that you can do amazing things for His kingdom.

2) Your Interests

Put Him first by inviting Him into anything and everything that you're interested in. Anything that you're passionate about—invite Him into that space. Don't just put Him in that spirituality box.

1 Corinthians 10 says it like this: "So whether you eat or drink or whatever you do, do it all for the glory of God." *Whatever* you do, you are to do it for God. And practice this with other people.

3) Your Relationships

If you want to put God first, especially as a young person, please choose your friends carefully. Because you'll become like whomever you are spending the most time with. I'm not saying put up walls and live in a Christian bubble, but the people who are closest to you should be the people who share your values and your vision of God. Choose friends who will push you in the right direction. In John 13:34, Jesus says, "A new command I give you: Love one another." Jesus is referring to the Church, the people of God. He said, "As I have loved you, so you must love one another. By this, everyone will know that you are my disciples, if you love one another."

It's possible you have been hurt or betrayed by Christians in your life. But Jesus says, "Here's what I want you to do. I want you to have so much love for each other that people look at you and say, 'They must know Jesus.'"

Can someone look at your life and be wowed by the forgiveness and grace you display, just by how you treat your brothers and sisters in Christ? Can they see that you are Jesus's disciple by your love, your patience, and your forbearance for them? Remember that your position of freedom in Him becomes a witness to your brothers and sisters who long for that same freedom. So, if your social circles are keeping you from that freedom, you may need to cut some relationships off and begin some new ones. That is how you live a God-first life.

4) Your Finances

Money tends to be an area we keep God out of. But if you want to guard your heart against false idols, put God first in your finances. Why is it that a $50 bill can look so big when the offering basket is passing by us, but can look so small when we're with our family at Chili's?

In Matthew 6:24, Jesus says, "No one can serve two masters. Either you will hate the one and love the other, or you will be devoted to the one and despise the other. You cannot serve both God and Money." The capital "M" is intentional because it represents the Greek word for the god of Money, called Mammon. Listen, when you put God first in your life, everything else will fall into place.

Proverbs 3:9 also says, "Honor the Lord with your wealth, with the firstfruits of all your crops." Here, he's referring to the tithe, the first 10 percent that belongs to Him. Why should we take that seriously? Because "then your barns will be filled to overflowing, and your vats will brim over with new wine." God says money is the number one test of your priorities. He says, "Give me the first and I'll bless the rest."

There's actually one thing God can't do: He can't be second. The theological term for this is called the preeminence of God. The preeminence of God means that God is above all more than all-in-all. So put God first in your finances. Honoring God with your money will actually open the windows of heaven to free you from financial stress. It's the reverse of what the world teaches us. That's how God's economy works.

5) Your Troubles

When you face unexpected problems and pressures, turn to God first, before you talk to your friend or your mom or your dad or your children. When the time of trouble comes, Psalm 50:15 says, "And call on me in the day of trouble; I will deliver you, and you will honor me."

As Joshua pronounced in 24:15, "... if serving the Lord seems undesirable for you, then choose for yourself this day whom you will serve," we must make a selection: Will we serve the gods of our forefathers, the gods of worldly culture that you've seen lead to destruction and death, or do you want to follow the God who makes all things new and has set aside a special treasure for you?

As for me and my house, we will serve the Lord.

STEP 8

USING SPIRITUAL WEAPONS FOR A SPIRITUAL WAR

The temptation to fixate on your past is a demonic attack. The temptation to live your life apart from your identity in Christ is a demonic attack. The temptation to eat from the wrong tree is a demonic attack. The temptation to bend to cultural pressures and carry on the curses that try and stick to you is a demonic attack. The temptation to incline your ear to the voice of the enemy and denounce the voice of God is a demonic attack. The temptation to forget God's promises and wring your hands in debilitating anxiety is a demonic attack.

You're either in the battle or in bondage.

You are in the middle of a war—a battle for your mind and your soul—whether you realize it or not. Pretending it's not happening does not make it any less real; it just makes you more susceptible to the lies and schemes of the enemy. You're either in the battle or in bondage. It's time to wake up! 1 Peter 5:8 (NLV) says, "Keep awake! Watch at all times. The devil is working against you. He is walking around like a hungry lion with his mouth open. He is looking for someone to eat."

We can't fight a spiritual war with weapons that we would use to fight in this world. We need to be armed for battle with spiritual weapons.

> *For though we live in the world, we do not wage war as the world does. The weapons we fight with are not the weapons of the world. On the contrary, they have divine power to demolish strongholds. We demolish arguments and every pretension that sets itself up against the knowledge of God, and we take captive every thought to make it obedient to Christ. —2 Corinthians 10:3-5*

There's a great line from the classic movie *The Untouchables* where Sean Connery mocks an attacker for "bringing a knife to a gunfight."[5] We do that all the time when we try to deal with spiritual issues with the tools offered by the world. And the first thing you need to know is that every problem you have is spiritual. This is why we can't handle worldly problems with worldly solutions. You may read better books, go to conferences, spend time with a therapist, take pills, and try the latest fad in a quest for ultimate health and wellness—but you're just taking a knife to a gunfight.

The enemy is skilled at turning footholds into strongholds.

---

5   Brian de Palma, *The Untouchables* (June 2, 1987; Hollywood, CA: Paramount Studios).

Any search for real-life solutions must begin with spiritual truth. In other words, God's Word. When we learn what He has to say, we are on our way to a big breakthrough. As I mentioned in chapter one, there is a particular biblical word that describes the prison of your past—*stronghold.*

This word, *stronghold*, contains the imagery of a castle or fortress. What it represents for us is an area of life where the enemy has captured territory and entrenched himself. Thinking and behavior become increasingly reflective of the stronghold.

The enemy is skilled at turning footholds into strongholds. That's how addiction happens, for example. It begins small—just a foothold. Then it takes over and becomes a stronghold. Any hope for a personal breakthrough must begin with learning how to root out the strongholds in our lives. Let me put it this way: A stronghold is a prison locked by deception.

Deception is a core strategy employed by the enemy. In John 8:44, Jesus exposes the true nature of the enemy, stating, "You belong to your father, the devil, and you want to carry out your father's desires. He was a murderer from the beginning, not holding to the truth, for there is no truth in him. When he lies, he speaks his native language, for he is a liar and the father of lies." This powerful verse highlights the enemy's nature as a deceiver and reinforces the importance of recognizing the lies and deceptive tactics used against us.

However, the Bible also reminds us of God's redemptive plan and His desire for our abundant life. In John 10:10, Jesus declares, "The thief comes only to steal and kill and destroy; I have come that they may have life, and have it to the full." This verse signifies the stark contrast between the enemy's intentions and the abundant life that Jesus offers.

The enemy's primary goal is to deceive and ultimately destroy, whereas Jesus came to bring life to its fullest expression.

Through deception, the enemy seeks to warp our perception of truth, veering us away from God's plan and His Word. Scripture constantly reminds us to stay alert and guard against deception. We need spiritual vigilance. We have to acknowledge that the enemy is continually seeking opportunities to deceive and lead us astray.

Jesus said in John 8:32, "Then you will know the truth, and the truth will set you free." We combat the lies of the enemy with God's truth. This truth will set us free. At this time, take the survey at the end of this chapter, "*Deception Versus Truth*". Prayerfully consider the lists in the three exercises and use the prayers at the end of each to confess any ways you have given in to deception. You can't instantly renew your mind, but the process will never start without acknowledging your mental strongholds and defense mechanisms.

You're in a battle and you need to dress for it.

When Jesus prayed just hours before he was arrested, He said: "Sanctify them in the truth; your word is truth" (John 17:17, ESV). Lies hold you back. Truth sets you free.

The lies of the enemy, even when they are deeply entrenched in our lives, must be overcome. In fact, the Bible says they can and must be *demolished*. The apostle Peter described His divine power this way:

His divine power has granted to us all things that pertain to life and godliness, through the knowledge of him who called us to his own glory and excellence, by which he has granted to us his precious and very great promises, so that through them you may become partakers of the divine nature, having escaped from the corruption that is in the world because of sinful desire. For this very reason, make every effort to supplement your faith with virtue, and virtue with knowledge, and knowledge with self-control, and self-control with steadfastness, and steadfastness with godliness, and godliness with brotherly affection, and brotherly affection with love. For if these qualities are yours and are increasing, they keep you from being ineffective or unfruitful in the knowledge of our Lord Jesus Christ.
—*2 Peter 1:3-8, ESV*

Peter made it quite clear that we are empowered for life change and breakthroughs by "his precious and very great promises." In other words—His Word. And the divine nature he wrote about is something very real and as available to us today in the twenty-first century as it was in the first century for blessed people who truly walk with Jesus.

Do you ever come home feeling beat and tell your spouse, "Man, it's been a battle today. I'm not sure who won." Some days, life just feels like such a struggle. And this really shouldn't surprise us because we *are* in a struggle. Paul tells us in Ephesians 6:10-11 to "Finally, be strong in the Lord and in his mighty power. Put on the full armor of God, so that you can take your stand against the devil's schemes." You don't usually wear armor if you're not expecting a fight.

But the struggle is not against your spouse. It's not against your boss. It's not against political figures. Paul says, "For our struggle is not against flesh and blood, but against the rulers, against the authorities, against the powers of this dark world and against the spiritual forces of evil in the heavenly realms" (v.12). There's a war going on—a really dark world—with spiritual forces of evil working against us.

And then there's this little phrase that is mentioned five times in the book of Ephesians alone, "in the heavenly realms." Paul seems to be indicating that there is a realm besides the realm you and I are living in right now, one that we can't see. You know it's true because you have sensed it. Things have happened in your life that just couldn't be explained. That's because the event was strategic. Paul says, "Therefore put on the full armor of God." You're in a battle and you need to dress for it.

I'm going to give you the armor in this chapter so that when—not if, but *when*—the day of evil comes, you'll be prepared. For there *is* a day of evil coming. We have to be prepared for it so that, as Paul says, ". . . when the day of evil comes, you may be able to stand your ground. And after you have done everything, to stand" (v. 13). So, let's learn how to fight the enemy with the right weapons. The more you fight with the wrong weapons, the more your enemy will back you into a corner and lock you up—and take the key with him.

God wants you to stop fighting your battle in the wrong realm and in the wrong areas—the things that you can only see in the flesh. You don't need to yell louder, manipulate more, or lie. You need to take control of the situation. God has given you different weapons to fight with than the weapons you are using. He's given you heavenly weapons. Earthly weapons won't cut it.

In Ephesians 5:11, Paul says, "Have nothing to do with the fruitless deeds of darkness, but rather expose them." Some of us are treating the reality of spiritual warfare far too lightly, and we need to examine ourselves to see how those fruitless deeds of darkness may be manifesting in our own lives. We need to expose the devil for who he is.

THE DEVIL IS REAL

The devil is not a *symbol* of evil, as some people believe. The devil is not a cosmic force. He's not a metaphor. He's not some nasty guy in a red jumpsuit with a pitchfork. The Bible tells us he's a person—more specifically—a fallen angel. The Bible actually records three angels by name in the Bible. The Bible talks about the angel Michael, the angel Gabriel, and the angel Lucifer. And all of them, at one point in time, were in heaven. And before any of the Bible stories ever unfolded, Satan rebelled and was cast out of heaven. And I believe, along with some Bible scholars, that Satan was cast out of heaven between Genesis 1:1 and Genesis 1:2. In the original text, there's a little punctuation mark in between those two phrases which denotes a passage in time. After Genesis 1:1, "In the beginning God created the heavens and the earth," there's a gap leading into verse 2, "now the Earth was formless and empty."

So, there was a destructive event that happened on earth that caused it to be formless and void because God wouldn't create something that is formless and void. God is perfect in all of His ways. He creates perfect things. Other Scriptures seem to provide evidence of this, as well, such as Isaiah 14:12-17 and Ezekiel 28.

Satan wanted to be worshiped, adored, and revered, just like God. God wasn't too fond of that idea. So, Lucifer lost his position in the heavenly realm. And Jesus was there at the right hand of the Father, the Eternal Son, and saw it happen. The Bible records this in Luke 10:18. Jesus said, "I saw Satan fall like lightning from heaven." God moved swiftly.

The casting out of Lucifer was recorded more fully in Revelation 12:7-8. It says that "... war broke out in heaven. Michael and his angels fought against the dragon, and the dragon and his angels fought back." BUT, "... he was not strong enough." See, Satan wants you to believe that he is stronger. The strength of the devil will *never*—and I mean NEVER—measure up to God's strength.

One third of the angels in heaven rebelled with Satan, and they lost their place in heaven with him. "The great dragon was hurled down— that ancient serpent called the devil, or Satan, who leads the whole world astray. He was hurled to the earth, and his angels with him" (v. 9).

So, he's operating right now in this realm. Perhaps that's why the earth became formless and void. And perhaps that's why he's trying to make your life formless and void. Perhaps he's trying to bring a Genesis 1:2 experience into your life where you become formless, with no purpose or identity. He wants to bring chaos and destruction to your life. The enemy is against you.

If you don't recognize who the enemy is, you'll fight the wrong battles.

John calls Satan "the ruler of this world" (John 12:31).

2 Corinthians 4:4 says that he is "the god of this age." Note the lowercase "g".

Ephesians 2:2 says he's "the prince of the power of the air."

1 John 5:19 says that "the whole world lies under the sway of the wicked one."

The names assigned to Satan illustrate that we are fighting a real entity, a real personality, with a lot of other real personalities in his army. We're not fighting an idea or a philosophy or a worldview. We have a real enemy who takes the time to personalize his attacks on us individually and personally.

THE DEVIL IS AT WAR WITH US

The devil is strategically scheming and devising a way to destroy you. He's working *right now*. He wants you to believe otherwise. It's called a psyop, or a psychological operation, and you'll become a *casualty* of war if you don't realize and accept that there is a war going on. And if you don't recognize who the enemy is, you'll fight the wrong battles. You'll wage war on the wrong battlefield. You'll continue fighting the wrong enemy. An awareness of the reality of what you cannot *see* is one of the best gifts you can have.

That's why in 1 Peter 5:8, the apostle says, "Be alert and of sober mind. Your enemy the devil prowls around like a roaring lion looking for someone to devour." This is a wake-up call. A lion doesn't give you an advanced warning of his attack. He hides. He goes undercover. He pounces at the right time, at the opportune time for *him*, and leaps on his prey. Just because you can't see it, doesn't mean it isn't real.

Above all, *don't be scared*. Resist him, standing firm in the faith. Remember, God Himself said, *"But he wasn't strong enough."* He's already lost, and he knows it. But even a pencil-necked loser can overcome a target who thinks he or she is in a playground instead of a battleground. You need to be aware that your enemy is lying in cover. He's waiting. Be alert.

When Jesus was led by the Spirit into the wilderness to be tempted, this was the only time in the Bible that is recorded that Satan actually confronted Jesus. Matthew 4 and Luke 4 both describe this "contest" between Jesus and Satan. There are a few things to note about this encounter. The devil didn't even try to mess with Jesus until He was alone, fasting and vulnerable. Jesus was out there in the wilderness without food, for forty days and forty nights. *Forty.* His objective was to "gotcha!" Jesus, to eject him from the kingdom of freedom into a kingdom that only paraded as free. That's a pretty dirty trick. The devil's not looking for a fair fight.

And he knows the scriptures. He's not afraid to use them, but he twists them. That's why it's so important for us to study and interpret scripture *by* scripture. If you only have a vague idea of what the Bible says, then he'll get away with the lie and you'll be wounded, dragging your way through life as a crippled soldier tethered to his sin. The word-by-word description of the devil's temptation of Jesus indicates that it was the *last* verbal exchange between them during those forty days. We have no idea what else the devil tried to tempt Him with during that period, but I think it's safe to say that Jesus always had scripture to counteract the devil's lies. It may be that this account was recorded for us as a tutorial for battling the enemy. Jesus fought fire with fire, scripture for scripture.

You have more control over what the enemy is taking from you and how much he is harassing you than you actually realize.

The Bible says in Luke 4:13 that when the devil had run out of ammunition, he left Jesus "until an opportune time." Since the devil is a lying coward, he ran off hoping for a *more* opportune time in the future. Rest assured he'll come at you again when you're at your weakest and when you're distracted by hunger or sorrow or even success—when you've let your guard down. You need to know that's how he operates. He's a knife in the dark when you're not looking.

Now, the truth is, the devil has power, but I don't believe a Christian can become possessed because when the Spirit of God lives in you—and that's what happens when you accept Jesus—the Bible says that the Spirit of God indwells you (See 1 Corinthians 3:16). If you are a temple of the Holy Spirit, how could you also house a demonic spirit? However, if we give him entry, Satan will use his power to harass, oppress, and attack. You *can* suffer greatly at the hands of the enemy.

But make no mistake—you have more control over what the enemy is taking from you and how much he is harassing you than you actually realize. In Ephesians 4:26, though not referring directly to spiritual warfare, Paul refers to anger, which speaks directly to how we give the enemy ammunition to use against us. He says, "In your anger, do not sin."

I mentioned in an earlier chapter that anger itself is not a sin. Jesus was angry when He cleared out the Temple, but his anger was directed toward the right thing; so He took the appropriate action. But if we take it too far, we have given the enemy permission to rule us. "... Do not let the sun go down while you are still angry, and do not give the devil a **foothold**" (v. 27, author emphasis). When you allow an emotion to lead to sin, you leave a crack in the window and the door ajar for the enemy to sneak in.

This does not mean that every time you sin or get angry that you've opened the door to the enemy and he's going to wreak havoc. It's unresolved sin that gives him the opportunity. Unresolved sin is what keeps you chained up.

That sounds like a lot of bad news. Let me give you some good news:

The Devil Is Subject to Our God

He trembles at our God. He's already had one pretty overwhelming encounter with our God, and that lasted a millisecond. And our God lives inside every single one of us. Anytime you align yourself with the God you serve, you become as victorious as God is over the devil. *Always* remember that the devil is only a fallen angel. He's not a fallen God. He is not Hector to God's Achilles. God's Achilles to a scorpion—an ugly, sharp-tailed bug that can be squashed underfoot—is a better comparison.

The devil is not omniscient; he can't read our minds (though he knows humanity pretty well by now). He's not omnipresent; as a spirit, he may be able to move pretty fast, but he's not everywhere at once. He's not all-powerful—not even close. He really only has as much power as we give him. His power is fear and lies—and he *is* really, really good at manipulation. He has no compunction, no conscience, about committing "crimes against humanity". That is his favorite hobby because God loves humanity; He designed us in His own image. The devil hates God and the only way he can hurt God is by hurting us. Satan is also astonishingly uncreative. He uses the same old methods of manipulation and the same old lies that he did thousands of years ago. All he can do is twist what God has created into ugly caricatures—if we let him. Think about the behavior of crabs when they are trapped in a bucket. When one tries to climb out toward freedom, the other crabs will pull it back down. This is what the devil does because HE isn't free. In fact, you could argue that he's the greatest prisoner of all. So, you better believe he will make every last-ditch effort to make you his cellmate for life.

Part of your Christianity is beautiful communion with God, but there's another part of your Christianity that is confrontation with the devil.

And that's why in 1 John 4:4, John says, "You, dear children, are from God and you have overcome them because the one who is in you is greater than the one who is in the world." That truth alone gives us ample reason to praise God right now. This battle is between God and a gaggle of no-longer-angelic losers that God has us training against. He's provided the armor and weapons, and He's not just training us from the back or on the sidelines; He's *in* us, every moment of the way. ". . . we are more than conquerors through him who loved us" (Romans 8:37).

God is the absolute authority on spiritual warfare. Remember Paul's directive to wage war with spiritual weapons, not worldly ones (2 Corinthians 10:3-4)? A spiritual war needs to be fought spiritually, with spiritual weapons, and we need to learn how to fight a spiritual war.

Part of your Christianity is beautiful communion with God, but there's another part of your Christianity that is confrontation with the devil. We cannot handle this with passivity. But we also have nothing to be afraid of. Stand your ground. Fight your fight. God has given us the war gear we need.

So, what weapons has God equipped us with to fight these ongoing spiritual battles?

THE NAME OF JESUS

Your first weapon is the name of Jesus. We intentionally sing songs about Jesus. We love the wonderful, powerful name of Jesus. Other names have power, too. Cancer is a powerful name. Anxiety is a powerful name. Debt is a powerful name. Addiction is a powerful name. Depression is a powerful name. But Philippians 2:9 (author emphasis) says, "Therefore God exalted him to the *highest place and gave him the name that is above every name . . .*"

Child of God, you've got a name you can wield that will evoke a response that no other name can. When you begin to use the name of Jesus with power, Philippians 2:10 continues, ". . . that at the name of Jesus, every knee should bow, in heaven and on earth and under the earth." That name works everywhere. ". . . and every tongue acknowledge that Jesus Christ is Lord, to the glory of God the Father" (v. 11).

Wielding this weapon is as simple as a child crying out for help. Paul tells us in Romans 10 to just call on His name. That's it. You sing the name, you worship the name, you declare the name. You shout the name of Jesus in every situation. For every wicked thing in your life—disease, addiction, debt, anxiety, depression—bring it into subjection to Jesus because it's the name above all names.

The best part is that the devils have to get in line. When you use this weapon, the name of Jesus, they respond with obedience because they *have* to. When you pray the name of Jesus over your own life and the lives of others, you have been covered with His banner of protection—instantly.

THE WORD OF GOD

The Word of God is a weapon of authority. Hebrews 4:12 says, "For the word of God is alive and active. Sharper than any double-edged sword . . ." All throughout scripture, we see the sword as the metaphor for the word of God. And a sword is an offensive weapon. The sword of the word of God is the only *offensive* weapon listed in the entire armor of God. Some of you are fighting and using weapons that you're not authorized to use—anger, intimidation, manipulation. But God has given you the most powerful weapon of all—the authority to speak the word of God to the heavenly realms.

Let's go back to Ephesians 6:13-17 and finish where we started:

> *After you have done everything, to stand. Stand firm then, with the belt of truth buckled around your waist, with the breastplate of righteousness in place, and with your feet fitted with the readiness that comes from the gospel of peace. In addition to all this, take up the shield of faith, with which you can extinguish all the flaming arrows of the evil one. Take the helmet of salvation and the sword of the spirit, which is the word of God.*

So you wrap yourself with truth; you ferret out and discard the lies of the enemy. You protect your heart with righteousness by being in right standing with God; you've confessed your sin, repented, and realigned with God. Your feet are shod with readiness that comes from the gospel of peace—in other words, you're willing to go wherever God wants you to go. Then, you take up the shield of faith, which you use to keep the lies of the enemy from reaching you. Your mind is protected by the salvation of Jesus Christ. And then you take up your only offensive weapon, the sword of the spirit, which is the very word of God.

Sounds like Jesus was giving us a foretaste of the power of this weapon in action after all in Matthew 4 and Luke 4! Every time the enemy tried to tempt Jesus with an easy way out, Jesus responded with

"*As it is written.*" The enemy uses scripture as a weapon, too. He swiped at Jesus with scripture he'd taken out of context, and Jesus responded to the enemy with more scripture, in context. This is why we need that belt of truth—because it will give us the insight we need to recognize the lie and strike back with the rightly divided word of God. Make it personal to you. Insert *"I"* as you declare the truth of the scriptures. There's no greater blow to the enemy than a person who knows that the truth is for *them*. He will have no other choice than to go fetch that key and let you go.

THE POWER OF THE CROSS OF JESUS

We can't forget about the power of the cross. His willingness to die for us on the cross is powerful enough, but there's even more power behind it than that. Paul says that between Friday, when He died on the cross, and Sunday, when he rose from the dead, Jesus descended to the lower parts of the earth. (See Ephesians 4:9.) Why? Because He was confronting our real enemy face-to-face. And he told him, "I have paid the sin debt. It is paid in full. Hand over the keys of death. They're mine."

The enemy has been disarmed. Because of the cross of Jesus Christ, there is nothing he can throw at you that would result in his victory. Jesus fully controls your fate now. That's what the keys symbolize. In Revelation 1:18, Jesus is talking to John the beloved, "I am the Living One; I was dead, and now look, I am alive forever and forever!" And because of this, the outcomes in our lives will always be victorious, even if they don't quite line up with what we expected.

Using your spiritual weapons, you are equipped to be victorious in the battle against demonic forces of evil. Using these weapons, you can practice these seven steps of spiritual warfare and breaking strongholds:

1) Identify the strongholds:

The first step in breaking strongholds is to identify the specific areas of your life where you feel trapped or entangled. This involves recognizing any sinful patterns, lies, or negative thought patterns that have taken hold in your life.

2) Confess and repent:

Once you have identified the strongholds, it is important to confess and repent of any sin that may have contributed to their formation. This involves acknowledging the ways in which you have cooperated with the enemy and aligning your heart and mind with God's truth.

3) Renounce lies and false beliefs:

In this step, you actively reject the lies and false beliefs that have been influencing your thinking and behavior. It involves renouncing the power that these lies have held over you and aligning your thoughts with God's truth and promises.

4) Replace with truth:

After renouncing the lies, it is important to replace them with God's truth. This involves renewing your mind with the Word of God, meditating on His promises, and allowing His truth to permeate your thoughts and beliefs.

5) Break ungodly soul ties:

Unhealthy and ungodly soul ties can contribute to strongholds in our lives. Breaking these ties involves severing any unhealthy and sinful connections with individuals who have influenced us negatively and establishing healthy boundaries in relationships.

6) Prayer and spiritual warfare:

Prayer is a powerful tool in breaking strongholds. Engaging in spiritual warfare, relying on the power of the Holy Spirit, and seeking God's guidance and protection are essential in the process of finding freedom.

7) Accountability and support:

It is important to have the support and accountability of fellow believers or a trusted counselor in the process of breaking strongholds. These individuals can provide encouragement, guidance, and prayer as you walk through the process and pursue lasting freedom.

For many, Revelation is a challenging book to understand. Here's the power behind the weapon of the cross. In Revelation 12:11, John describes the fight with our enemy, "And they have defeated him by the blood of the lamb and by their testimony." "They" is a reference to us—those who believe in Christ. So, what did the cross purchase for you? Your testimony. You were under a shroud of darkness, believing the lies of the enemy. But the cross of Jesus paid your debt and gave you a testimony of your own.

Sometimes, our victory feels like a lie, as we go around suffering loss after loss, betrayal after betrayal, hardship after hardship. It's almost like we are being talked out of the truth that the devil is powerless over us. So let me encourage you about the victory that you have over the devil. In Romans 8:35 (NLT), Paul says, "Does it mean he no longer loves us if we have trouble or calamity, or are persecuted, or hungry, or destitute, or in danger, or threatened with death?"

So yes, the fight may be hard, but "… in all these things, we are more than conquerors through him who loved us" (v. 37). So, my friends, you are more than a conqueror. Hardship doesn't prove the devil's power.

But God's power is revealed through the abundant grace at work within us *in the middle* of hardships.

Make this your life motto. Say it out loud daily. Look in the mirror and declare it like your life depends on it. Pretty soon you'll start believing it, and you will begin to experience what you have always been looking for—freedom.

DECEPTION VERSUS TRUTH

Take a few moments to read the following statements and check off the ones that are true for you.

WAYS I HAVE BEEN DECEIVED BY THE WORLD

- ❏ Believing that having an abundance of money and possessions will make me happy (Matthew 13:22; 1 Timothy 6:10)
- ❏ Believing that eating food, drinking alcohol, or using drugs can relieve my stress and make me happy (Proverbs 23:19-21)
- ❏ Believing that an attractive body, phony personality, or image will meet my needs for acceptance and significance (Proverbs 31:10; 1 Peter 3:3-4)
- ❏ Believing that gratifying sexual lust will bring lasting satisfaction without any negative consequences (Ephesians 4:22; 1 Peter 2:11)
- ❏ Believing that I can sin and suffer no negative consequences (Hebrews 3:12-13)
- ❏ Believing that I need more than Jesus to meet my needs of acceptance, security, and significance (2 Corinthians 11:2-4,13-15)
- ❏ Believing that I can do whatever I want regardless of others and still be free (Proverbs 16:18; Obadiah 3; 1 Peter 5:5)
- ❏ Believing that people who refuse to receive Jesus will go to heaven anyway (1 Corinthians 6:9-11)

❑ Believing that I can associate with bad company and not become corrupted (1 Corinthians 15:33-34)

❑ Believing that I can read, see, or listen to anything and not be corrupted (Proverbs 4:23-27; Matthew 5-28)

❑ Believing that there are no earthly consequences for my sin (Galatians 6:7-8)

❑ Believing that I must gain the approval of certain people in order to be happy (Galatians 1:10)

❑ Believing that I must measure up to certain religious standards in order for God to accept me (Galatians 3:2-3; 5:1)

❑ Believing that there are many paths to God and Jesus is only one of the many ways (John 14:6)

❑ Believing that I must live up to worldly standards in order to feel good about myself (1 Peter 2:1-12)

Dear Heavenly Father, I confess that I have been deceived by [confess the items you checked above]. I thank You for Your forgiveness, and I choose to believe Your Word and believe in Jesus who is the Truth. In Jesus's name I pray. Amen.

WAYS I HAVE DECEIVED MYSELF

❑ Hearing God's Word but not doing what it says (James 1:22)

❑ Saying I have no sin (1 John 1:8)

❑ Thinking I am something or someone I'm really not (Galatians 6:3)

❑ Thinking I am wise in this worldly age (1 Corinthians 3:18-19)

❑ Thinking I can be truly religious and not control what I say (James 1:26)

❑ Thinking that God is the source of my problems (Lamentations 3:1-24)

❑ Thinking I can live successfully without the help of anyone else (1 Corinthians 12:14-20)

Dear Heavenly Father, I confess that I have deceived myself by [confess the items checked above]. Thank You for Your forgiveness. I commit myself to believe only Your truth. In Jesus's name I pray. Amen.

WAYS I HAVE WRONGLY DEFENDED MYSELF

❑ Denial of reality (conscious or unconscious)

❑ Fantasy (escaping reality by daydreaming, TV, movies, music, computer or video games, drugs, or alcohol)

❑ Emotional insulation (withdrawing from people or keeping people at a distance to avoid rejection)

❑ Regression (reverting back to less threatening times)

❑ Displaced anger (taking out frustrations on innocent people)

❑ Projection (attributing to another what you find unacceptable in yourself)

❑ Rationalization (making excuses for my own poor behavior) or lying (protecting self through falsehoods)

❑ Hypocrisy (presenting a false image)

Dear Heavenly Father, I confess that I have wrongly defended myself by [confess the items checked above]. Thank You for Your forgiveness. I trust You to defend and protect me. In Jesus's name I pray. Amen.

The wrong ways we have employed to shield ourselves from pain and rejection are often deeply ingrained in our lives.

You may need additional discipling/counseling to learn how to allow Jesus to be your rock, fortress, deliverer, and refuge (see Psalm 18:1-2). The more you learn how loving, powerful, and protective God is, the more you'll be likely to trust Him. The more you realize how much God unconditionally loves and accepts you, the more you'll be released to be open, honest, and vulnerable (in a healthy way) before God and others.

The New Age movement has twisted the concept of faith by teaching that we make something true by believing it. That is false. We cannot create reality with our minds; only God can do that. Our responsibility is to face reality and choose to believe what God says is true. True biblical faith, therefore, is choosing to believe and act upon what is true, because God has said it is true, and He is the Truth. Faith is something you decide to do, not something you feel like doing.

Believing something doesn't make it true; it's already true, therefore we choose to believe it! Truth is not conditioned by whether we choose to believe it or not.

Everybody lives by faith. The only difference between Christian faith and non-Christian faith is the object of our faith. If the object of our faith is not trustworthy or real, then no amount of believing will change that. That's why our faith must be grounded on the solid rock of God's perfect, unchanging character and the truth of His Word.

CONNECT WITH JASON

To learn more visit

JasonHanash.com

@PASTORJASONHANASH

Printed in the USA
CPSIA information can be obtained
at www.ICGtesting.com
JSHW011948261123
52466JS00005B/7